GH00374298

Presented To:

_____

Presented By:

_____

Date:

_____

GOD's Little Lessons on
Life
for
Mothers

eagle

Guildford

Originally published by Honor Books, Tulsa, Oklahoma, USA. This edition published by Eagle, an imprint of Inter Publishing Service (IPS) Ltd, PO Box 530, Guildford, Surrey GU2 5FH.

British Library Cataloguing in Publication Data.. A catalogue record for this book is available from the British Library.

Devotions drawn from original manuscripts prepared by W. B. Freeman Concepts, Inc., Tulsa, Oklahoma. Edited by Kelli James.

Scripture quotations are as follows:
AMP – *The Amplified Bible*, Old Testament. © 1965 by Zondervan Publishing House, Grand Rapids, Michigan. New Testament copyright © 1958 by The Lockman Foundation, La Habra, California. Used by permission.
CEV – *The Contemporary English Version*, © 1995 by the American Bible Society. All rights reserved.
KJV – *King James Version* of the Bible.
NASB – *New American Standard Bible.* © 1960, 1962, 1963, 1968, 1971, 1972, 1973, 1975, 1977 by The Lockman Foundation. Used by permission.
NIV – *New International Version* © 1973, 1978, 1984 by International Bible Society. Used by permission of Zondervan Publishing House. All rights reserved.
NKJV – The *New King James Version* of the Bible. © 1979, 1980, 1982, 1994 by Thomas Nelson, Inc., Publishers. Used by permission.
NLT – *New Living Translation*, © 1996. Used by permission of Tyndale House Publishers, Inc., Wheaton, Illinois 60189. All rights reserved.
NRSV – *New Revised Standard Version* © by the Division of Christian Education of the National Council of the Churches of Christ in the USA, 1989.
The Message – *The Message: New Testament with Psalms and Proverbs* ©1993, 1994, 1995 by Eugene H. Peterson. Published by NavPress, Colorado Springs, Colorado. Used by permission.
RSV – *The Revised Standard Version Bible*, © 1952 by the Division of Christian Education of the Churches of Christ in the United States of America used by permission.

Typeset by Eagle
Printed by Cox & Wyman, Reading
ISBN No: 0 86347 287 7

Introduction

Mothers face many challenging situations every day. In the midst of running children to school, going to work, cleaning the house and taking children to practices and lessons, we have many opportunities to become stressed, angry or discouraged. But God's Word is filled with the answers we need to help us overcome every problem we encounter in the course of a day.

However, busy mums need an easily accessible source for those answers. *God's Little Lessons on Life for Mothers* is a storehouse of wisdom and direction packaged in a mum-friendly format. It not only contains relevant Scripture quotations that cover a wide range of topics, but a devotional story that helps apply the scriptures to real-life situations.

God's Word is for you. He desires that you know His love, His peace and His mercy. He wants you to grow in His grace, His wisdom and His strength. He wants to provide you with His comfort, His encouragement and His protection. As you read the following pages, our prayer is that you would come to know God more, for in Him are all the answers for life.

Table of Contents

GOD's Little Lessons on Life for Mothers:

Anger

A gentle response defuses anger, but a sharp tongue kindles a temper-fire.

Proverbs 15:1 The Message

Whoever is slow to anger has great understanding, but one who has a hasty temper exalts folly.

Proverbs 14:29 NRSV

He who is slow to anger is better than the mighty, and he who rules his spirit than he who takes a city.

Proverbs 16:32 NKJV

When angry, do not sin; do not ever let your wrath, your exasperation, your fury or indignation, last until the sun goes down.

Ephesians 4:26 AMP

Anger

A Reason to Laugh

Peggy was nervous about the forthcoming dinner party she and her husband were hosting. It was their first time to have guests for dinner since the birth of their son, Pete. Adding to Peggy's tension was the fact that one of the guests was her husband Bill's new supervisor.

Sensing the tension in his parents, the baby became irritable and fussy, which only increased Peggy's frustration. In an attempt to comfort little Pete, Peggy picked him up, raised him high over her head and kissed his bare tummy. To her surprise, he smiled and giggled – the first genuine laughter she had heard from her young son.

In an instant, the evening took on an entirely new tenor. Peggy became more relaxed and baby Pete relaxed as well. The dinner party was a great success.

Can the laughter of a small child change a day? Yes! So can laughter shared between adults or a chuckle prompted by the memory of a funny event.

When you're feeling 'stressed out', don't allow yourself to explode in anger. Get alone if you have to, but find a reason to laugh, and watch the frustration melt away!

Anger

Do your best to live at peace with everyone.

Romans 12:18 CEV

But now you must rid yourselves of all such things as these: anger, rage, malice, slander and filthy language from your lips.

Colossians 3:8 NIV

Bridle your anger, trash your wrath, cool your pipes – it only makes things worse.

Psalm 37:8 The Message

For we know Him Who said, Vengeance is Mine [retribution and the meting out of full justice rest with Me]; I will repay [I will exact the compensation], says the Lord.

Hebrews 10:30 AMP

Anger

Where Anger Leads

Susan was deeply disappointed by the lack of emotional closeness she felt in her marriage. Consequently, she began to lash out at her husband. He, of course, reacted with his own defensive anger. Over time their anger grew and eventually the threat of divorce became an often-used weapon in their confrontations. Finally, Susan's husband moved out, and she filed for divorce.

The divorce proceedings were bitter. They fought all the way through it. When they met to sign the final papers, they stopped to look at each other and Susan saw in his eyes the very feelings she was experiencing – a feeling of longing, yet resignation. She thought, *I don't want to divorce him, and I don't think he wants to divorce me.*

She voiced her thoughts to her husband, and for a moment it appeared he might also soften and admit he too still cared. Instead, he said in a dull monotone, 'We've come this far, I guess we should finish it.' Susan left the courtroom realizing she had never really wanted a divorce. She just wanted her husband to listen.

Don't allow anger to lead you anywhere, especially down a road you truly don't want to travel.

Assurance

I wipe away your sins because of who I am. And so, I will forget the wrongs you have done.

Isaiah 43:25 CEV

As far as sunrise is from sunset, he has separated us from our sins.

Psalm 103:12 The Message

All that the Father gives me will come to me, and whoever comes to me I will never drive away.

John 6:37 NIV

Most assuredly, I say to you, he who hears My word and believes in Him who sent Me has everlasting life, and shall not come into judgment, but has passed from death into life.

John 5:24 NKJV

Assurance

Hope from the Flowers

The fictional character Sherlock Holmes is known for his keen powers of observation in solving crimes. But Holmes also used his skills for renewing his faith. In *The Adventure of the Naval Treaty*, Dr Watson says of Holmes: 'He walked past the couch to an open window and held up the drooping stalk of a moss rose, looking down at the dainty blend of crimson and green. It was a new phase of his character to me, for I had never before seen him show an interest in natural objects.

'"There is nothing in which deduction is so necessary as in religion," said he, leaning with his back against the shutters ... "Our highest assurance of the goodness of Providence seems to me to rest in the flowers. All other things, our powers, our desires, our food, are really necessary for our existence in the first instance. But this rose is an extra. Its smell and its colour are an embellishment of life, not a condition of it. It is only goodness which gives extras, and so I say again that we have much to hope from the flowers."'

Life is filled with these 'extras' – gifts from a loving God that enrich our lives and assure us of His great love.

Assurance

For by grace you have been saved through faith;
and this is not of your own doing, it is the gift
of God.

Ephesians 2:8 RSV

And I am sure that God, who began the good
work within you, will continue his work until it
is finally finished on that day when Christ Jesus
comes back again.

Philippians 1:6 NLT

I am the good shepherd; I know my sheep and
my sheep know me – just as the Father knows
me and I know the Father – and I lay down my
life for the sheep.

John 10:14–15 NIV

God affirms us, making us a sure thing in
Christ, putting his Yes within us. By his Spirit
he has stamped us with his eternal pledge – a
sure beginning of what he is destined to complete.

2 Corinthians 1:21–22 The Message

Assurance

God Is Always Near

In *Love and Duty,* Anne Purcell writes about seeing Major Jim Statler standing with her pastor outside his study after a Sunday service. She knew instantly that he was there with news about her husband, Ben, who was on active duty in Vietnam. Jim had chilling news: 'He was on a helicopter that was shot down ... he's missing in action.'

Anne recalls, 'Somewhere in the back of my mind, a little candle flame flickered. This tiny flame was the vestige of my faith.' Days passed without word. To her, being the wife of an MIA was like being caught in limbo. She found herself able to pray only one thing: 'Help me, dear Father.' She says, 'I hung onto this important truth – that He would help me – and the flickering flame of my candle of faith began to grow.' For five years, Anne Purcell clung to the fact that God was near. Little did she know that during those years before she was reunited with her husband, he was whispering to her from a POW cell, 'Anne, find solace and strength in the Lord.'

God *is* always near. In every circumstance, He's right there beside you saying, 'Rest in the assurance of My strength and love.'

Children

'Let the children come to me. Don't stop them!
For the Kingdom of God belongs to such as
these.'

Mark 10:14 NLT

Don't you see that children are God's best gift?
The fruit of the womb his generous legacy? Like
a warrior's fistful of arrows are the children of
a vigorous youth. Oh, how blessed are you
parents, with your quivers full of children!

Psalm 127:3–4 The Message

Her children arise and call her blessed.

Proverbs 31:28 NIV

When a woman is about to give birth, she is in
great pain. But after it is all over, she forgets the
pain and is happy, because she has brought a
child into the world.

John 16:21 CEV

Children

Mother's Anchor

Henry Ward Beecher, considered by many to be one of the most effective and powerful pulpit orators in the history of the United States, not only had a reputation for having an extremely sensitive heart, but also for having a great love of the sea. Many of his sermons were laced with loving anecdotes with a seafaring flavour.

Beecher once said, 'Children are the hands by which we take hold of heaven.' And he had this to say about a mother's relationship with her child:

'A babe is a mother's anchor. She cannot swing far from her moorings. And yet a true mother never lives so little in the present as when by the side of the cradle. Her thoughts follow the imagined future of her child. That babe is the boldest of pilots, and guides her fearless thoughts down through scenes of coming years. The old ark never made such voyages as the cradle daily makes.'

What a wonderful image to think of a child as being on a voyage from heaven, through life, to return to heaven's port one day. What a challenge to think that our children have not come along to join us in our sail through life, but we are to join in their voyage!

Children

For this child I prayed, and the LORD has granted me my petition which I asked of Him. Therefore I also have lent him to the LORD; as long as he lives he shall be lent to the LORD.

1 Samuel 1:27–28 NKJV

All your sons will be taught by the LORD, and great will be your children's peace.

Isaiah 54:13 NIV

Only take heed, and guard your life diligently, lest you forget the things which your eyes have seen and lest they depart from your [mind and] heart all the days of your life. Teach them to your children and your children's children.

Deuteronomy 4:9 AMP

Point your kids in the right direction – when they're old they won't be lost.

Proverbs 22:6 The Message

Children

The Attitude Diet

Several years ago, a man was asked to give a speech at a graduation ceremony. After he had finished, he sat on the platform watching the graduates receive their college degrees. Suddenly, the entire audience began applauding a student who had earned a perfect degree. During the applause, a faculty member seated next to the speaker leaned over and said to him, 'She may be Miss Genius, but her attitude stinks.' The speaker later said, 'Without even thinking, my hands stopped clapping in mid-air. I couldn't help but think, *How sad.*'

No matter how beautiful, intelligent, talented, or athletic a child may be, there's no substitute for a positive, loving attitude towards others! The foremost architects of that attitude are not a child's teachers or pastor, but the parents.

Be aware of the attitudes you 'feed' your children every day. They are the diet of your child's mind, just as food is the diet of your child's body. Don't feed your children junk ideas, sour opinions, rotten theology, poisoned feelings or wilted enthusiasm. Instead, feed them the best and most positive ideas, emotional expressions and thoughtful opinions you have!

Comfort

Blessed be the God and Father of our Lord Jesus Christ, the Father of mercies and God of all comfort; who comforts us in all our affliction so that we may be able to comfort those who are in any affliction with the comfort with which we ourselves are comforted by God.

2 Corinthians 1:3–4 NASB

But the Comforter, which is the Holy Ghost, whom the Father will send in my name, he shall teach you all things, and bring all things to your remembrance, whatsoever I have said unto you.

John 14:26 KJV

The LORD is good, a refuge in times of trouble. He cares for those who trust in him.

Nahum 1:7 NIV

Come to me, all who labour and are heavy laden, and I will give you rest.

Matthew 11:28 RSV

Comfort

Comforting Retreat

Have you ever explored a tidal pool? Low tide is the perfect time to find a myriad of creatures that have temporarily washed ashore from the depths of the sea.

Children are often amazed that they can pick up these shelled creatures and stare at them eye to eye. The creatures rarely exhibit any form of overt fear, such as moving to attack or attempting to scurry away. They simply withdraw into their shells, instinctively knowing they are safe as long as they remain in their strong, cosy shelters.

Likewise, we are safe when we remain in Christ. We are protected from the hassles of life and the fear of the unknown. Those things will come against us, much like the fingers of a brave and curious child try to invade the sea creature's shell, but they have no power to harm us when we retreat into the shelter of Christ.

The Lord commanded us to learn to *abide* in Him and to *remain* steadfast in our faith. He tells us to *trust* in Him absolutely, and to *shelter* ourselves under His strong wings and in the cleft of His rock-like presence. He delights when we *retreat* into His arms for comfort and tender expressions of love.

Comfort

God's a safe-house for the battered, a sanctuary during bad times.

Psalm 9:9 The Message

Though I am surrounded by troubles, you will preserve me against the anger of my enemies.

Psalm 138:7 NLT

Wait for the LORD; be strong and take heart and wait for the LORD.

Psalm 27:14 NIV

We share in the terrible sufferings of Christ, but also in the wonderful comfort he gives.

2 Corinthians 1:5 CEV

Comfort

Talk to God

In the midst of her intense grief, Betty found it very difficult to pray. She was drowning in a sea of turbulent emotions and hardly knew her own name, much less what to request from God.

One afternoon, a friend of Betty's came by and soon Betty was pouring all of her hurts, fears and struggles out to her. She admitted she was angry with God and disappointed that her prayers for her husband's healing weren't answered. She admitted she was having difficulty believing God would do anything for her – in the present or the future. Finally, as the well of her emotions began to run dry, Betty's friend said quietly, 'I have only one piece of advice to give you. Let's talk to God.'

Betty's friend put her arms around her and prayed a simple, heartfelt prayer. After she had finished, she said, 'Christ is with you. He is in you. And where He is, because of Who He is, He heals.'

No matter what you may be going through today, your best recourse is to invite Jesus Christ to manifest Himself in you and through you. He gives you Himself and in Him is all the power, strength, encouragement, love and comfort you need.

Commitment

As you therefore have received Christ Jesus the Lord, so walk in Him, rooted and built up in Him and established in the faith, as you have been taught, abounding in it with thanksgiving.

Colossians 2:6–7 NKJV

With all these things in mind, dear brothers and sisters, stand firm and keep a strong grip on everything we taught you both in person and by letter.

2 Thessalonians 2:15 NLT

Commit your way to the LORD; trust in him and he will do this: He will make your right-eousness shine like the dawn, the justice of your cause like the noonday sun.

Psalm 37:5–6 NIV

So if you find life difficult because you're doing what God said, take it in stride. Trust him. He knows what he's doing, and he'll keep on doing it.

1 Peter 4:19 The Message

Commitment

Commit to Hope

Anita Septimus has worked as a social worker for HIV-infected children since 1985. In the first few months she worked with her tiny clients, three of them died. Despair began to overwhelm her. She made a commitment to stick with the job for three more months, during which time she could not get a friend's words out of her thoughts, 'You have not chosen a pretty profession.'

She had to admit her friend was right. It took resolve to accept that fact and simply do what she could to help families make the most of what remained of their children's lives. She is still there.

Over the last ten years, her clinic has grown considerably. Today, Anita and her staff care for more than 300 families with AIDS children. They go into their homes, teach infection prevention and help parents plan for the future.

One AIDS baby wasn't expected to see her first birthday, but she recently celebrated her tenth. Such 'long-term' clients give back to Anita what she terms 'an indestructible sense of hope' – a precious gift!

When you make a commitment to sow hope into the lives of others, you will reap back tremendous hope for your own life.

Commitment

Therefore devote yourselves completely to the LORD our God, walking in his statutes and keeping his commandments, as at this day.

1 Kings 8:61 NRSV

Commit your work to the LORD, and then your plans will succeed.

Proverbs 16:3 NLT

Now all has been heard; here is the conclusion of the matter: Fear God and keep his commandments, for this is the whole duty of man.

Ecclesiastes 12:13 NIV

Turn your back on evil, work for the good and don't quit. God loves this kind of thing, never turns away from his friends.

Psalm 37:27 The Message

Commitment

Hull House

Jane was only seven years old when she visited a shabby street in a nearby town, and seeing ragged children there, announced that she wanted to build a big house so poor children would have a place to play. As a young adult, Jane and a friend visited Toynbee Hall in London, where they saw educated people helping the poor by living among them.

She and her friend returned to Chicago, restored an old mansion, and moved in! There they cared for children of working mothers and held sewing and cooking classes. Older boys and girls had clubs at the mansion. An art gallery and public music, reading and craft rooms were created in the mansion. Her dream came true!

Jane didn't stop there. She spoke up for people who couldn't speak for themselves. She was eventually awarded an honorary degree from Yale. President Theodore Roosevelt dubbed her 'America's most useful citizen', and she was awarded the Nobel Prize for Peace.

No matter how famous she became, however, Jane Addams remained a resident of Hull House. She died there, in the heart of the slum she had come to call home.

When we commit our dreams and plans to the Lord, He will see to it that they come to pass.

Confidence

So we are always confident, knowing that while we are at home in the body we are absent from the Lord. For we walk by faith, not by sight.

2 Corinthians 5:6–7 NKJV

Let us then approach the throne of grace with confidence, so that we may receive mercy and find grace to help us in our time of need.

Hebrews 4:16 NIV

We have confidence to enter the holy place by the blood of Jesus.

Hebrews 10:19 NASB

For the LORD shall be your confidence, firm and strong, and shall keep your foot from being caught [in a trap or some hidden danger].

Proverbs 3:26 AMP

Confidence

Always Useful to God

In *Glorious Intruder*, Joni Eareckson Tada writes about Diane, who suffers from multiple sclerosis: 'In her quiet sanctuary, Diane turns her head slightly on the pillow toward the corkboard on the wall. Her eyes scan each thumbtacked card and list. Each photo. Every torn piece of paper carefully pinned in a row. The stillness is broken as Diane begins to murmur. She is praying.

'Some would look at Diane – stiff and motionless – and shake their heads ... "What a shame. Her life has no meaning. She can't really do anything." But Diane is confident, convinced her life is significant. Her labor of prayer counts. She pushes back the kingdom of darkness that blackens the alleys and streets of east Los Angeles. She aids homeless mothers, single parents, abused children, despondent teenagers, handicapped boys, and dying and forgotten old people. Diane is on the front lines, advancing the gospel of Christ, holding up weak saints, inspiring doubting believers, energizing other prayer warriors, and delighting her Lord and Savior.'

What a difference we can make, regardless of our situation in life, if we have confidence in God's desire to use us. God is willing and able to use us regardless of our ability or inability – He always has a plan!

Confidence

Trust the LORD! Be brave and strong and trust the LORD.

Psalm 27:14 CEV

Beloved, if our heart does not condemn us, we have confidence before God.

1 John 3:21 NASB

And I am sure that God, who began the good work within you, will continue his work until it is finally finished on that day when Christ Jesus comes back again.

Philippians 1:6 NLT

Be strong in the Lord [be empowered through your union with Him]; draw your strength from Him [that strength which His boundless might provides].

Ephesians 6:10 AMP

Confidence

You Are What You Think You Are

The story is told of a man who found an eagle's egg and put it into the nest of a farmyard chicken. The eaglet hatched with the brood of chicks and grew up with them. All his life, the eagle did what the chickens did. It scratched the dirt for seeds and insects to eat. It clucked and cackled. And it flew no more than a few feet off the ground, in a chicken-like thrashing of wings and flurry of feathers.

One day the eagle saw a magnificent bird far above him in the cloudless sky. He watched as the bird soared gracefully on the wind, gliding through the air with scarcely a beat of its powerful wings.

'What a beautiful bird,' the young eagle said. 'What is it called?'

The chicken next to him said, 'Why, that's an eagle – the king of all birds. But don't think about him. You could never be like him.'

So the young eagle returned to pecking the dirt for seeds, and it died thinking it was a chicken.

What you think of your own potential not only defines who you are today, but what you will be tomorrow. Find your confidence and strength in God and soar like the eagle!

Conflict

I appeal to you, brethren, by the name of our
Lord Jesus Christ, that all of you agree and that
there be no dissensions among you, but that
you be united in the same mind and the same
judgment.

1 Corinthians 1:10 RSV

And a servant of the Lord must not quarrel but
be gentle to all.

2 Timothy 2:24 NKJV

Hot tempers start fights; a calm, cool spirit
keeps the peace.

Proverbs 15:18 The Message

See that no one pays back evil for evil, but
always try to do good to each other and to
everyone else.

1 Thessalonians 5:15 NLT

Conflict

One of the Ten

The story is told of a couple at their golden wedding anniversary celebration. Surrounded by her children, grandchildren and great grandchildren, the wife was asked the secret to a long and happy marriage. With a loving glance towards her husband, she answered: 'On my wedding day, I decided to make a list of ten of my husband's faults which, for the sake of our marriage, I would overlook. I figured I could live with at least ten faults.'

A guest asked her to identify some of the faults she had chosen to overlook. Her husband looked a bit troubled at the thought of having his foibles and flaws revealed to the assembled group. However, his wife sweetly replied, 'To tell you the truth, dear, I never did get around to listing them. Instead, every time my husband did something that made me hopping mad, I would simply say to myself, *Lucky for him that's one of the ten.*'

Even the most devoted friends and spouses will experience storms in their relationships from time to time. Some conflicts are worth addressing in order to resolve them. Others are best left unspoken. With time, those issues that are truly of little importance tend to blow past without any need for a 'blowup'.

Conflict

How good and pleasant it is when brothers live together in unity!

Psalm 133:1 NIV

May the God of steadfastness and encouragement grant you to live in such harmony with one another, in accord with Christ Jesus, that together you may with one voice glorify the God and Father of our Lord Jesus Christ.

Romans 15:5–6 RSV

Always keep yourselves united in the Holy Spirit, and bind yourselves together with peace.

Ephesians 4:3 NLT

God loves you and has chosen you as his own special people. So be gentle, kind, humble, meek, and patient.

Colossians 3:12 CEV

Conflict

How to Fight Fair

Author Charlie W. Shedd shares 'Our Seven Official Rules for a Good, Clean Fight' in the book he wrote to his daughter, *Letters to Karen*. They are:

1. Before we begin we must both agree that the time is right.
2. We will remember that our only aim is deeper understanding.
3. We will check our weapons often to be sure they're not deadly.
4. We will lower our voices one notch instead of raising them two.
5. We will never quarrel or reveal private matters in public.
6. We will discuss an armistice whenever either of us calls 'halt'.
7. When we have come to terms, we will put it away till we both agree it needs more discussing.

Says Shedd, 'No small part of the zest in a good marriage comes from working through differences. Learning to zig and zag with the entanglements; studying each other's reactions under pressure; handling one another's emotions intelligently – all these offer a challenge that simply can't be beat for sheer fun and excitement.'

Resolving conflict 'sheer fun and excitement'? Sounds pretty far-fetched! But if we follow these rules, we can learn to use conflict to grow closer together instead of letting it wedge us further apart.

Courage

Be strong, and let your heart take courage, all
you who wait for the LORD.

Psalm 31:24 NRSV

Be strong and courageous, do not fear or be dis-
mayed . . . for the one with us is greater than the
one with him.

2 Chronicles 32:7 NASB

I command you – be strong and courageous! Do
not be afraid or discouraged. For the LORD your
God is with you wherever you go.

Joshua 1:9 NLT

In all these things we are more than conquerors
through him who loved us.

Romans 8:37 NIV

Courage

Speak Out and Stand Up

While he was a pastor in Indianapolis, Henry Ward Beecher preached a series of sermons about gambling and drunkenness. He soundly denounced the men of the community who profited by these sins.

The next week, a would-be assailant accosted Beecher on the street. Brandishing a pistol, the man demanded that Beecher make some kind of retraction about what he had said the previous Sunday.

'Take it back, right here!' he demanded with an oath, 'or I will shoot you on the spot!'

Beecher calmly replied, 'Shoot away!' The man was taken aback by his response. Beecher just walked away, saying over his shoulder as he left the scene, 'I don't believe you can hit the mark as well as I did!'

Courage is more than just having convictions. As mothers, we must have the courage to stand up to the world and its ways and say 'no'. Courage requires being willing to speak and to act in order to bring about change. We must stand firm in our convictions when our children pipe up, 'Everybody else does it!'

With courage from God our Father, we can make an impact – in our own lives, in our families, in our neighbourhoods, in our cities and ultimately, in our nation.

Courage

Wait for the LORD; Be strong, and let your heart take courage; Yes, wait for the LORD.

Psalm 27:14 NASB

So you should not be like cowering, fearful slaves. You should behave instead like God's very own children, adopted into his family – calling him 'Father, dear Father.'

Romans 8:15 NLT

Light, space, zest – that's God! So, with him on my side I'm fearless, afraid of no one and nothing.

Psalm 27:1 The Message

'The Lord helps me! Why should I be afraid of what people can do to me?'

Hebrews 13:6 CEV

Courage

Be Strong and Courageous

Napoleon called Marshall Ney the bravest man he had ever known. Yet Ney's knees trembled so badly one morning before a battle that he had difficulty mounting his horse. When he was finally in the saddle, he shouted contemptuously down at his limbs, 'Shake away, knees. You would shake worse than that if you knew where I am going to take you.'

Courage is not a matter of not being afraid. It is a matter of taking action even when you are afraid!

Courage is more than sheer bravado – shouting, 'I can do this!' and launching out with a do-or-die attitude over some reckless dare.

True courage is manifest when a person chooses to take a difficult or even dangerous course of action, simply because it is the right thing to do. Courage is looking beyond yourself to what is best for another.

The source of all courage is the Holy Spirit, our Comforter. It is His very nature to remain at our side, helping us. When we welcome Him into our lives and He compels us to do something, we can confidently trust He will be right there helping us accomplish whatever task He has called us to.

Deliverance

Because he cleaves to me in love, I will deliver him; I will protect him, because he knows my name. When he calls to me, I will answer him; I will be with him in trouble, I will rescue him and honor him.

Psalm 91:14–15 RSV

For he has rescued us from the one who rules in the kingdom of darkness, and he has brought us into the Kingdom of his dear Son.

Colossians 1:13 NLT

The Lord knows how to rescue godly men from trials and to hold the unrighteous for the day of judgment.

2 Peter 2:9 NIV

He who trusts in his own heart is a fool, But whoever walks wisely will be delivered.

Proverbs 28:26 NKJV

Deliverance

The Thundering Legion

The Militine Legion was one of the two most famous legions in the Roman army. It was also known as the Thundering Legion. The nickname was given by the philosopher-emperor Marcus Aurelius in AD 176, during a military campaign against the Germans.

In their march northwards, the Romans were encircled by precipitous mountains, which were occupied by their enemies. In addition, due to a drought they were tormented by great thirst. Then a member of the Praetorian Guard informed the emperor that the Militine Legion was made up of Christians who believed in the power of prayer. Although he himself had been a great persecutor of the Church, the emperor said, 'Let them pray then.' The soldiers bowed on the ground and earnestly sought God to deliver them in the name of Jesus Christ.

They had scarcely risen from their knees when a great thunderstorm arose. The storm drove their enemies from their strongholds and into their arms, where they pleaded for mercy. The storm also provided water to drink and ended the drought. The emperor renamed them the 'Thundering Legion', and subsequently abated some of his persecution of the Christians in Rome.

God is always ready and able to deliver us. We must simply trust Him.

Deliverance

When the righteous cry for help, the LORD hears, and delivers them out of all their troubles.

Psalm 34:17 RSV

Oh, the joys of those who are kind to the poor. The LORD rescues them in times of trouble.

Psalm 41:1 NLT

The LORD is my rock and my fortress and my deliverer; My God, my strength, in whom I will trust.

Psalm 18:2 NKJV

I call to the LORD, who is worthy of praise, and I am saved from my enemies.

Psalm 18:3 NIV

Deliverance

In the Very Hour

During World War II, a missionary family lived near a place where the Japanese tortured and killed their captives. Twice, the father was taken captive, then released unharmed. The third time the officer said to the missionary's wife, 'He has been returned to you two times – don't think he will be spared a third time.'

After she had put her five children to bed, the wife began a prayer vigil. At four o'clock, she awoke her children to join her, saying, 'The burden has become so heavy I cannot bear it alone.' A short while later, they heard footsteps approaching – ones she recognized as those of her husband!

Safely inside their home, he told her what had happened. He had been the last in a row of ten men. A Japanese soldier had gone down the row, slashing off the head of each man with a sword. Just as he raised his sword to kill the missionary, the officer shouted, 'Stop!' Then he roared to the missionary, 'Go home. Quick, get out of here!' He pushed the missionary past the guard and towards the gate. 'I looked at my watch,' the missionary said. 'It was 4 am.'

When we call to the Lord, we are saved from our enemies.

Discipline

I discipline my body and bring it into subjection, lest, when I have preached to others, I myself should become disqualified.

1 Corinthians 9:27 NKJV

I have been crucified with Christ; and it is no longer I who live, but Christ lives in me; and the life which I now live in the flesh I live by faith in the Son of God, who loved me, and delivered Himself up for me.

Galatians 2:20 NASB

He that hath no rule over his own spirit is like a city that is broken down, and without walls.

Proverbs 25:28 KJV

Clothe yourselves with the Lord Jesus Christ, and do not think about how to gratify the desires of the sinful nature.

Romans 13:14 NIV

Discipline

All We Did

Once upon a time there was a little boy who was given everything he wanted. As an infant, he was given a bottle at the first little whimper. He was picked up and held whenever he fussed. His parents said, 'He'll think we don't love him if we let him cry.'

He was never disciplined for leaving the garden, even after being told not to. He suffered no consequence for breaking windows or tearing up flowerbeds. His parents said, 'He'll think we don't love him if we stifle his will.'

His mother picked up after him and made his bed. His parents said, 'He'll think we don't love him if we give him chores.'

Nobody ever stopped him from using bad words. He was never reprimanded for scribbling on his bedroom wall. His parents said, 'He'll think we don't love him if we stifle his creativity.'

He never was required to go to Sunday school. His parents said, 'He'll think we don't love him if we force religion down his throat.'

One day the parents received news that their son was in jail on a felony charge. They cried to each other, 'All we ever did was love him and do things for him.' Unfortunately, that is, indeed, *all* they did.

Discipline

Blessed is the man whom God corrects; so do not despise the discipline of the Almighty.

Job 5:17 NIV

Happy are those whom you discipline, O LORD, and whom you teach out of your law.

Psalm 94:12 NRSV

For I am with you and will save you, says the LORD... But I must discipline you; I cannot let you go unpunished.

Jeremiah 30:11 NLT

As many as I love, I rebuke and chasten. Therefore be zealous and repent.

Revelation 3:19 NKJV

Discipline

Godly Discipline

A grandfather once found his grandson, Joey, jumping up and down in his playpen, crying at the top of his voice. When Joey saw his grandfather, he stretched out his chubby hands and cried all the louder, 'Out, Gamba, out!'

Naturally, the grandfather reached down to lift Joey out, but as he did, Joey's mother said, 'No, Joey, you are being punished – so you must stay in your playpen.'

The grandfather felt at a loss as to what to do. On the one hand, he knew he must comply with the mother's efforts to discipline her son. On the other hand, Joey's tears and uplifted hands tugged at his heart. Love found a way! If Gamba couldn't take his grandson out of the playpen, he could climb in and join him there!

Discipline, in its finest form, is 'directing a child towards a better way'. Discipline goes beyond punishment by instilling the desire never to repeat the misdeed, and instead, make a better choice. The desire to do right is born of love – the love of the child for the parent, and more importantly, the love of the parent shown to the child.

God disciplines us, but He never leaves us. He is always right there in it with us.

Discontentment

Out of heaven He let you hear His voice, that
He might instruct you.

Deuteronomy 4:36 NKJV

Godliness actually is a means of great gain,
when accompanied by contentment.

1 Timothy 6:6 NASB

Do not let your heart envy sinners, but always
continue in the fear of the LORD. Surely there is
a future, and your hope will not be cut off.

Proverbs 23:17–18 NRSV

Search for the LORD and for his strength, and
keep on searching. Think of the wonderful
works he has done, the miracles, and the judgments he handed down.

1 Chronicles 16:11 NLT

Discontentment

Money, Money, Money

In 1923, eight of the most powerful money magnates in the world gathered for a meeting at the Edgewater Beach Hotel in Chicago, Illinois. The combined resources and assets of these eight men tallied more than the US Treasury that year. In the group were: Charles Schwab, president of a steel company; Richard Whitney, president of the New York Stock Exchange; and Arthur Cutton, a wheat speculator. Albert Fall was a presidential cabinet member, a personally wealthy man. Jesse Livermore was the greatest Wall Street 'bear' in his generation. Leon Fraser was the president of the International Bank of Settlements, and Ivan Krueger headed the largest monopoly in the nation.

What happened to these men in later years? Schwab died penniless. Whitney served a life sentence in Sing Sing Prison. Cutton became insolvent. Fall was pardoned from a federal prison so he might die at home. Fraser, Livermore and Krueger committed suicide. Seven of these eight extremely rich men ended their lives with nothing.

Money is certainly not the answer to discontentment. Only God can give us peace, contentment and joy. When we focus on God and His goodness in our lives, whether we have money or not, we can live content, knowing that God is our gracious Provider.

Discontentment

Keep your lives free from the love of money,
and be content with what you have; for he has
said, 'I will never leave you or forsake you.'

Hebrews 13:5 NRSV

I have learned in whatever state I am, to be content: I know how to be abased, and I know how
to abound. Everywhere and in all things I have
learned both to be full and to be hungry, both
to abound and to suffer need. I can do all things
through Christ who strengthens me.

Philippians 4:11–13 NKJV

We know that God causes all things to work
together for good to those who love God, to
those who are called according to His purpose.

Romans 8:28 NASB

He who dwells in the shelter of the Most High
will rest in the shadow of the Almighty.

Psalm 91:1 NIV

Discontentment

Thankfully Content

In *Little Women*, Mrs March tells this story to
her daughters:

'Once upon a time, there were four girls,
who had enough to eat and drink and wear, a
good many comforts and pleasures ... and yet
they were not contented. ... These girls ... made
many excellent resolutions; but they ... were
constantly saying, "If we only had this," or "If we
could only do that.." ... So they asked an old
woman what spell they could use to make them
happy, and she said, "When you feel discontent-
ed, think over your blessings, and be grateful."

'They decided to try her advice, and soon
were surprised to see how well off they were.
One discovered that money couldn't keep
shame and sorrow out of rich people's houses;
another that ... she was a great deal happier
with her youth, health, and good spirits than a
certain fretful, feeble old lady, who couldn't
enjoy her comforts; a third that, disagreeable as
it was to help get dinner, it was harder still to
have to go begging for it; and the fourth, that
even carnelian rings were not so valuable as
good behavior.'

Remember that discontentment is rooted in
ungratefulness. Teach your children the secret
of contentment by teaching them to be thankful.

Failure

If the LORD delights in a man's way, he makes his steps firm; though he stumble, he will not fall, for the LORD upholds him with his hand.

Psalm 37:23–24 NIV

For whatever is born of God overcomes the world. And this is the victory that has overcome the world – our faith.

1 John 5:4 NKJV

The steadfast love of the LORD never ceases, his mercies never come to an end; they are new every morning; great is thy faithfulness.

Lamentations 3:22 RSV

Give us help for the hard task; human help is worthless. In God we'll do our very best; he'll flatten the opposition for good.

Psalm 60:12 The Message

Failure

Starting Over

In 1991, Anne Busquet was General Manager of the Optima Card division for American Express. When five of her 2,000 employees were found to have hidden $24 million in losses, she was held accountable. Busquet had to face the fact that, because she was an intense perfectionist, she apparently came across as intimidating and confrontational to her subordinates – so much so, they were more willing to lie than to report bad news to her!

Busquet lost her Optima job, but was given a second chance by American Express: an opportunity to salvage one of its smaller businesses. Her self-esteem shaken, she nearly turned down the offer. However, she decided this was her chance to improve the way she related to others. She took on the new job as a personal challenge to change.

Realizing she had to be much more understanding, she began to work on being more patient and listening more carefully and intently. She learned to solicit bad news in a reassuring way.

Four years after she was removed from her previous position, Anne Busquet was promoted to an executive vice-president position at American Express.

Failure is not the end; it is a teacher for a new beginning and a better life!

Failure

If God is for us, who can be against us? He who did not spare his own Son, but gave him up for us all – how will he not also, along with him, graciously give us all things?

Romans 8:31–32 NIV

Now thanks be to God who always leads us in triumph in Christ, and through us diffuses the fragrance of His knowledge in every place.

2 Corinthians 2:14 NKJV

All of us have sinned and fallen short of God's glory. But God treats us much better than we deserve, and because of Christ Jesus, he freely accepts us and sets us free from our sins.

Romans 3:23–24 CEV

God-loyal people don't stay down long; soon they're up on their feet, while the wicked end up flat on their faces.

Proverbs 24:16 The Message

Failure

Giving God All

Janette Oke, a best-selling novelist with more than forty books to her credit, is considered the modern-day 'pioneer author' for Christian fiction. When she first decided to write, she said to God, 'Lord, I'm going to write this book. If it works, and if I discover I have talent, I'll give it all to You.'

Janette sensed God was not pleased with the bargain she was trying to strike with Him. She felt in her heart as if He was responding, 'If you're serious about this, then I want everything before you start.' Thus she gave Him her ambitions and dreams, and trusted Him with the outcome of her efforts. She left it up to Him to teach her, whether she was successful or not. And a shelf of novels later, Janette Oke has proven 'God can teach spiritual truths through fictional characters'.

The greatest step of faith is to trust God *before* we see the results of our efforts. Whether we fail or succeed, God will still be with us. God doesn't ask for our best, He asks us for ourselves. When we give Him everything He can use even our failures to bring us to eventual success.

Faith

What is faith? It is the confident assurance that what we hope for is going to happen. It is the evidence of things we cannot yet see.

Hebrews 11:1 NLT

With all of these, take the shield of faith, with which you will be able to quench all the flaming arrows of the evil one.

Ephesians 6:16 NRSV

We walk by faith, not by sight.

2 Corinthians 5:7 NKJV

'Everything is possible for him who believes.'

Mark 9:23 NIV

Faith

Trust God for His Best

Author Elizabeth Elliot writes in *A Lamp for My Feet* about a game she played as a young girl. She writes, 'My mother or father would say, "Shut your eyes and hold out your hand." That was the promise of some lovely surprise. I trusted them, so I shut my eyes instantly and held out my hand. Whatever they were going to give me I was ready to take.' She continues, 'So should it be in our trust of our heavenly Father. Faith is the willingness to receive whatever He wants to give, or the willingness not to have what He does not want to give.'

Several months before Christmas, Jared begged his mother to buy him a new bicycle just like his friend's – now! His mother was single, however, and there was no extra money for a new bicycle until Christmas.

Jared's friend generously lent him his bicycle to ride, and the longer Jared rode it, the more he realized it really wasn't the right bicycle for him.

How often do we think God has forgotten us, when He's merely giving us time to understand what we really want so He can bring us His best?

Faith

... for in Christ Jesus you are all children of God through faith.

Galatians 3:26 NRSV

And now, just as you accepted Christ Jesus as your Lord, you must continue to live in obedience to him.

Colossians 2:6 NLT

Every child of God can defeat the world, and our faith is what gives us this victory.

1 John 5:4 CEV

As the body without the spirit is dead, so faith without deeds is dead.

James 2:26 NIV

Faith

Faith Like a Child

Some years ago, a boy in a small Florida town heard that the Russians were our enemies. He began to wonder about the Russian children, finding it hard to believe they were his enemies, too. He wrote a short note: 'Dear Comrade in Russia, I am seven years old and I believe that we can live in peace. I want to be your friend, not your enemy. Will you become my friend and write to me?'

He ended the letter 'Love and Peace' and signed his name. He then neatly folded the note, put it into an empty bottle and threw it into an inland lake near his home. Several days later, the bottle and note were retrieved on a nearby beach. A story about the note appeared in a local newspaper and a wire service picked up the story and sent it nationwide. A group of people from New Hampshire who were taking children to the Soviet Union as ambassadors of peace read the article, contacted the boy and his family and invited them to go with them. The little boy and his father travelled to Moscow as peacemakers!

Jesus told us to have faith like a little child. One boy believed he could make a difference, do you?

Family

'A man leaves his father and mother and is joined to his wife, and the two are united into one.'

Ephesians 5:31 NLT

Children, obey your parents in the Lord, for this is right. 'Honour your father and mother' – which is the first commandment with a promise ...

Ephesians 6:1–2 NIV

You must be very careful not to forget the things you have seen God do for you. Keep reminding yourselves, and tell your children and grandchildren as well.

Deuteronomy 4:9 CEV

Anyone who neglects to care for family members in need repudiates the faith. That's worse than refusing to believe in the first place.

1 Timothy 5:8 The Message

Family

'You're Special!'

While on holiday in New England, Sue and Kevin bought two red 'You're Special' plates at a shopping centre. They liked them so much they decided to use them as their 'everyday dishes'. Then one day, one of the plates broke. That night, Kevin said, 'You should get the special plate tonight.' 'Why?' Sue asked. 'Because you finished that big project that you were working on.'

The next night, Sue insisted that Kevin dine from the 'You're Special' plate, in honour of the help he had given to a neighbour in need. From then on, Sue and Kevin vied nightly for the honour of awarding the plate to the other.

When the plate finally broke, Sue said sadly, 'I had never been affirmed as much in my entire life as I was those eight months. What seemed like courtesy the first night Kevin gave me the plate actually set a precedent for our encouraging each other on a daily basis.'

There are many little things you can do every day to make your family feel special. Encouraging them on a daily basis sets a tone of warmth, peace and comfort in your home. Think of ways to make each member of your family feel special today.

Family

The wife does not have authority over her own body, but the husband does; and likewise also the husband does not have authority over his own body, but the wife does.

1 Corinthians 7:4 NASB

If anyone says, 'I love God,' yet hates his brother, he is a liar. For anyone who does not love his brother, whom he has seen, cannot love God, whom he has not seen. And he has given us this command: Whoever loves God must also love his brother.

1 John 4:20–21 NIV

How wonderful, how beautiful, when brothers and sisters get along!

Psalm 133:1 The Message

For the one who sanctifies and those who are sanctified all have one Father. For this reason Jesus is not ashamed to call them brothers and sisters.

Hebrews 2:11 NRSV

Family

A Picture-Perfect Christmas

During the Depression, many families could scarcely afford the bare essentials, much less Christmas presents. 'But, I'll tell you what we can do,' a father said to his six-year-old son, Pete. 'We can use our imaginations and make pictures of the presents we would like to give each other.'

For the next few days, each member of the family worked secretly, but joyfully. On Christmas morning, huddled around a scraggly tree decorated with a few pitiful decorations, the family gathered to exchange the presents they had created. And what gifts they were! Daddy got a shiny black limousine and a red motor boat. Mum received a diamond bracelet and new hat. Little Pete had fun opening his gifts, a drawing of a swimming pool and pictures of toys cut from magazines.

Then it was Pete's turn to give his present to his parents. With great delight, he handed them a brightly coloured crayon drawing of three people – man, woman and little boy. They had their arms around one another and under the picture was one word: US. Even though other Christmases were far more prosperous for this family, no Christmas in the family's memory stands out as more precious than the year they discovered their greatest gift was each other.

Favour

For surely, O LORD, you bless the righteous; you surround them with your favour as with a shield.

Psalm 5:12 NIV

A good name is to be chosen rather than great riches, Loving favor rather than silver and gold.

Proverbs 22:1 NKJV

They did not conquer the land with their swords; it was not their own strength that gave them victory. It was by your mighty power that they succeeded; it was because you favored them and smiled on them.

Psalm 44:3 NLT

When you find me, you find life, real life, to say nothing of God's good pleasure.

Proverbs 8:35 The Message

Favour

Your Reputation Precedes You

Roger was a good employee – not spectacular – but reliable, punctual, even-tempered and always willing to go the extra mile.

Brian also did good work, but he didn't mind cutting a few corners to finish a job, or leaving work a few minutes early to attend to his personal needs.

When Mr Jones, their supervisor, announced that one of the two men would be promoted, Roger counted on his record and his reputation to win him the post. Brian lobbied hard for the job in an underhand fashion by telling several of his co-workers that Roger had stolen credit for his innovative cost-saving measures, had misappropriated supplies and was known to overextend his lunch hour. He was careful, of course, to preface all of his remarks by saying, 'Just between the two of us . . .'

The following week, when Mr Jones announced that Roger had received the promotion, he received a rousing applause from his fellow employees. No one was surprised – except Brian, of course. After all, Roger's reputation had preceded him.

So had Brian's.

When we seek to walk in integrity towards God and others, God causes others to see us through His eyes of favour.

Favour

Never let loyalty and kindness get away from
you! Wear them like a necklace; write them
deep within your heart. Then you will find
favor with both God and people, and you will
gain a good reputation.

Proverbs 3:3–4 NLT

And Jesus grew in wisdom and stature, and in
favour with God and men.

Luke 2:52 NIV

But God was with him and delivered him out
of all his troubles, and gave him favor and wisdom in the presence of Pharaoh, king of Egypt;
and he made him governor over Egypt and all
his house.

Acts 7:9–10 NKJV

Fools don't care if they are wrong, but God is
pleased when people do right.

Proverbs 14:9 CEV

Favour

The Favour of God

The story is told of a king who owned a valuable diamond, one of the rarest and most perfect in the world. One day the diamond fell and a deep scratch marred its face. The king summoned the best diamond experts in the land to correct the blemish, but they all agreed they could not remove the scratch without cutting away a good part of the surface, thus reducing the weight and value of the diamond.

Finally one expert appeared and assured the king that he could fix the diamond without reducing its value. His confidence was convincing and the king gave the diamond to the man. In a few days, the artisan returned the diamond to the king, who was amazed to find that the ugly scratch was gone, and in its place a beautiful rose was etched. The former scratch had become the stem of an exquisite flower!

Any mistake we make in life may temporarily mar our reputation. But if we stick to what we know is right and continue to attempt to conform our will to that of God, we can trust Him to turn the 'scratches' on our souls into part of His signature – that's what it means to have God's favour.

Fear

Do not fear, for I am with you, do not be afraid, for I am your God; I will strengthen you, I will help you, I will uphold you with my victorious right hand.

Isaiah 41:10 NRSV

God's Spirit doesn't make cowards out of us. The Spirit gives us power, love, and self-control.

2 Timothy 1:7 CEV

'Peace I leave with you; my peace I give you. I do not give to you as the world gives. Do not let your hearts be troubled and do not be afraid.'

John 14:27 NIV

When I am afraid, I put my trust in you. O God, I praise your word. I trust in God, so why should I be afraid? What can mere mortals do to me?

Psalm 56:3–4 NLT

Fear

Overcoming Fear

When Beth's boss asked her to take on an extra project, Beth saw the opportunity to prove she could handle greater responsibility. She immediately began to think how she might approach the task and her enthusiasm ran high. But when the time came to start the project, Beth found herself telling her boss she was too busy to do it justice. The project was given to someone else, who earned a promotion for completing it successfully. Beth didn't receive any new opportunities and eventually took a position with another firm.

What had kept Beth from doing the project? Simple procrastination. She put off getting started on the job until she was paralysed with fear – fear that she might not be able to do the job or that her performance would not meet her boss's expectations. In the end, she didn't move ahead and thus reinforced her fears with a bigger sense of insecurity about her own ability.

If you find yourself procrastinating, ask God to show you how to overcome your fear, then do what He says. He wants you to succeed and live a fulfilled life, but you must step out in faith – He's waiting to bless you!

Fear

Do not be not afraid of sudden panic, or of the storm that strikes the wicked; for the LORD will be your confidence and will keep your foot from being caught.

Proverbs 3:25–26 NRSV

When you go through deep waters and great trouble, I will be with you. When you go through rivers of difficulty, you will not drown! When you walk through the fire of oppression, you will not be burned up; the flames will not consume you.

Isaiah 43:2 NLT

Yea, though I walk through the valley of the shadow of death, I will fear no evil; for You are with me; Your rod and Your staff, they comfort me.

Psalm 23:4 NKJV

You, LORD, are the light that keeps me safe. I am not afraid of anyone. You protect me, and I have no fears.

Psalm 27:1 CEV

Fear

Calm at the Core

In *Especially for a Woman,* Beverly LaHaye writes about how upset she was when her husband, Tim, told her he wanted to take flying lessons. Tim asked her to pray about the matter, but she writes, 'I started right off giving God my opinions and drawing my own conclusions. My fear ... was controlling me.' Tim suggested, 'Be open with the Lord. Let Him know you're afraid of flying, but that you're willing to be changed if that's what He would have.'

Beverly did just that. Tim took flying lessons, and she repeatedly committed her fears – and their lives – to the Lord.

Years later, she was a passenger in a commuter plane that was caught in a storm. As the plane bounced in the sky, the LaHayes' attorney – normally a very calm man – was sure they were going to crash. He looked over and saw that Beverly was asleep! He asked her later, 'How could you sleep so peacefully?'

Beverly responded, 'It had to be God. Only He could have brought me from that crippling fearfulness ... to a place where I could fly through such a storm and be at peace.'

When we let go of our fears, God will replace them with His peace.

Forgiveness

If we confess our sins, He is faithful and just to forgive us our sins and to cleanse us from all unrighteousness.

1 John 1:9 NKJV

In him we have redemption through his blood, the forgiveness of our trespasses, according to the riches of his grace which he lavished upon us.

Ephesians 1:7–8 RSV

As far as the east is from the west, so far has he removed our transgressions from us.

Psalm 103:12 NIV

I acknowledged my sin to You, and my iniquity I did not hide. I said, I will confess my transgressions to the Lord [continually unfolding the past till all is told] then You [instantly] forgave me the guilt and iniquity of my sin.

Psalm 32:5 AMP

Forgiveness

Forgiveness and Trust

Lisa was shocked when she discovered that David had run up thousands of pounds on every one of their credit cards. Not only was she furious about the mountain of debt, she was frustrated with herself for not recognizing David's compulsive spending habits.

In the days that followed, she wondered if she could ever trust her husband again and whether they would ever be able to get out of debt.

Rather than wait for something to happen, she took two bold steps. The first was to convince David he needed help, and the second was to seek out a financial planner. She learned if she carefully monitored the family funds, they could be out of debt in a few years. This brought hope for their financial future, and for the future of their marriage.

Another turnaround in their marriage came when David asked Lisa to forgive him. She found that forgiving David freed her to turn away from the matter of money and to focus on their relationship. She decided it was possible to love someone even though they had 'messed up'. Forgiving made trust possible again, and once trust was reestablished, their marriage began to heal.

Forgiveness turns the heart away from what was and is, to what can be.

Forgiveness

If you forgive those who sin against you, your heavenly Father will forgive you.

Matthew 6:14 NLT

Whenever you stand praying, forgive, if you have anything against anyone; so that your Father also who is in heaven may forgive you your transgressions.

Mark 11:25–26 NASB

Love your enemies, do good, and lend, hoping for nothing in return.

Luke 6:35 NKJV

Bear with each other and forgive whatever grievances you may have against one another. Forgive as the Lord forgave you.

Colossians 3:13 NIV

Forgiveness

Broken Silence

Meredith was surprised to receive a letter from her brother, Tim. It had been three years since she had spoken to him, even though they lived in the same town. In the letter, Tim told her he and his wife were expecting twins and he hoped she would come to visit the babies after they were born. He expressed his sorrow that they had not communicated more and apologized for whatever it was he had done to cause them to become estranged.

Meredith's initial reaction was one of anger. 'Whatever it was?' Didn't he know? She immediately sat down and wrote a five-page letter detailing all the things Tim had done to hurt her. When she read her letter, however, she was horrified by what she found.

She had thought she was being very matter-of-fact, but her words were full of anger and pain. Tears of forgiveness filled her eyes. Perhaps it wasn't all Tim's fault.

You may not even realize you're harbouring past hurts until something comes along to expose your pain. But when you forgive and release your hurts into God's hands, He can cleanse your heart and mind with His love and forgiveness and give you the power to forgive.

Friendship

Two are better than one; because they have a good reward for their labour. For if they fall, the one will lift up his fellow.

Ecclesiastes 4:9–10 KJV

A friend loves at all times, and a brother is born for adversity.

Proverbs 17:17 RSV

Wounds from a friend are better than many kisses from an enemy.

Proverbs 27:6 NLT

There are friends who pretend to be friends, but there is a friend who sticks closer than a brother.

Proverbs 18:24 RSV

Friendship

Winning Friends

Dale Carnegie, author of *How To Win Friends and Influence People,* is considered one of the greatest 'friend winners' of the century. He taught, 'You can make more friends in two months by becoming interested in other people than you can in two years by trying to get other people interested in you.'

To illustrate his point, Carnegie would tell how dogs have learned the fine art of making friends better than most people. When you get within ten feet of a friendly dog, he will begin to wag his tail, a visible sign that he welcomes and enjoys your presence. If you take time to pet the dog, he will become excited, lick you and jump all over you to show how much he appreciates you. The dog became man's best friend by being genuinely interested in people!

One of the foremost ways, of course, in which we show our interest in others is to listen to them – to ask questions, intently listen to their answers, and ask further questions based upon what they say. The person who feels 'heard' is likely to seek out his friendly listener again and again, and to count that person as a great friend.

Friendship

Share each other's troubles and problems, and in this way obey the law of Christ.

Galatians 6:2 NLT

Whoever loves his brother [believer] abides (lives) in the Light, and in It or in him there is no occasion for stumbling or cause for error or sin.

1 John 2:10 AMP

Your friend, and your father's friend, do not forsake.

Proverbs 27:10 RSV

Greater love has no one than this, than to lay down one's life for his friends.

John 15:13 NKJV

Friendship

Love Believes the Best

One of the noblest friendships in literature is that of Melanie and Scarlett in Margaret Mitchell's classic, *Gone with the Wind*. Melanie is characterized as a woman who 'always saw the best in everyone and remarked kindly upon it'. Even when Scarlett tries to confess her shameful behaviour towards Ashley, Melanie's husband, Melanie says, 'Darling, I don't want any explanation . . . Do you think I could remember you walking in a furrow behind that Yankee's horse almost barefooted and with your hands blistered – just so the baby and I could have something to eat – and then believe such dreadful things about you? I don't want to hear a word.'

Melanie's refusal to believe or even hear ill of Scarlett leads Scarlett to passionately desire to keep Melanie's high opinion. It is as Melanie lies dying that Scarlett faces her deep need for Melanie's pure and generous friendship: 'Panic clutching at her heart, she knew that Melanie had been her sword and her shield, her comfort and her strength.' In two words, Melanie had been her true friend.

A friend loves at all times and always believes the best. Is that the kind of friend you want to have? Is that the kind of friend you aspire to be?

Gossip

'Do not spread slanderous gossip among your
people.'

Leviticus 19:16 NLT

The words of a whisperer are like dainty
morsels, And they go down into the innermost
parts of the body.

Proverbs 18:8 NASB

Stay away from gossips – they tell everything.

Proverbs 20:19 CEV

A perverse man stirs up dissension, and a gossip
separates close friends.

Proverbs 16:28 NIV

Gossip

Gossip Golden?

Laura Ingalls Wilder writes in *Little House in the Ozarks*, 'I know a little band of friends that calls itself a woman's club. There is no obligation, and there are no promises; but in forming the club and in selecting new members, only those are chosen who are kind-hearted and dependable as well as the possessors of a certain degree of intelligence and a small amount of that genius which is the capacity for careful work. In short, those who are taken into membership are those who will make good friends, and so they are a little band who are each for all and all for each . . .

'They are getting so in the habit of speaking good words that I expect to see them all develop into Golden Gossips.

'Ever hear of golden gossip? I read of it some years ago. A woman who was always talking about her friends and neighbors made it her business to talk of them, in fact, never said anything but good of them. She was a gossip, but it was "golden gossip". This woman's club seems to be working in the same way.'

Who wouldn't enjoy belonging to such a club?

Gossip

A gossip betrays a confidence, but a trustworthy man keeps a secret.

Proverbs 11:13 NIV

Where there is no wood, the fire goes out; and where there is no talebearer, strife ceases.

Proverbs 26:20 NKJV

Their words are like an open pit, and their tongues are good only for telling lies.

Romans 3:13 CEV

Post a guard at my mouth, God, set a watch at the door of my lips.

Psalm 141:3 The Message

Gossip

The Untamed Tongue

Many analogies have been given for the 'untamed tongue'. Quarles likened it to a drawn sword that takes a person prisoner: 'A word unspoken is like the sword in the scabbard, thine; if vented, thy sword is in another's hand.'

Others have described evil speaking as:

- A freezing wind – one that seals up the sparkling waters and kills the tender flowers and shoots of growth. In similar fashion, bitter and hate-filled words bind up the hearts of men and cause love to cease to flourish.
- A fox with a firebrand tied to its tail, sent out among the standing corn just as in the days of Samson and the Philistines. So gossip spreads without control or reason.
- A pistol fired in the mountains, the echo of which is intensified until it sounds like thunder.
- A snowball that gathers size as it rolls down a mountain.

Perhaps the greatest analogy, however, is one given by a little child who came running to her mother in tears. 'Did your friend hurt you?' the mother asked.

'Yes,' said the girl. 'Where?' asked her mother.

'Right here,' said the child, pointing to her heart.

Ask God to place a watch over your tongue. Your words have the power to hurt and tear down, but they also have the power to heal and build up.

Guidance

For this God is our God for ever and ever; he will be our guide even to the end.

Psalm 48:14 NIV

The human mind plans the way, but the LORD directs the steps.

Proverbs 16:9 NRSV

Stalwart walks in step with God; his path blazed by God, he's happy.

Psalm 37:23 The Message

The LORD says, 'I will guide you along the best pathway for your life. I will advise you and watch over you.'

Psalm 32:8 NLT

Guidance

The Guide

In *A Slow and Certain Light,* Elisabeth Elliot
writes: 'When I lived in the forest of Ecuador I
usually traveled on foot.... Trails often led
through streams and rivers, but sometimes
there was a log high above the water which we
had to cross.

'I dreaded those logs and was always tempted to take the steep, hard way down into the
ravine and up the other side. But the Indians
would say, "Just walk across, senorita," and over
they would go, light-footed and confident. I was
barefoot as they were, but it was not enough.
On the log, I couldn't keep from looking down
at the river below. I knew I would slip. I had
never been any good at balancing myself ... so
my guide would stretch out a hand, and the
touch of it was all I needed. I stopped worrying
about slipping. I stopped looking down at the
river or even at the log and looked at the guide,
who held my hand with only the lightest touch.
When I reached the other side, I realized that if
I had slipped he could not have held me. But his
being there and his touch were all I needed.'

God is your guide.

Guidance

Then he led forth his people like sheep, and
guided them in the wilderness like a flock.

Psalm 78:52 RSV

For all who are being led by the Spirit of God,
these are sons of God.

Romans 8:14 NASB

He guides me in paths of righteousness for his
name's sake.

Psalm 23:3 NIV

When the Spirit of truth comes, he will guide
you into all truth. He will not be presenting his
own ideas; he will be telling you what he has
heard. He will tell you about the future.

John 16:13 NLT

Guidance

A Light for our Path

Benjamin Franklin came to a personal conclusion that the lighting of streets would not only add gentility to his city, but also make it safer. In seeking to interest the people of his native Philadelphia in street lighting, however, he didn't try to persuade them by *talking* about it. Instead, he hung a beautiful lantern on a long bracket outside his own front door. Then he kept the glass brightly polished, and diligently lit the wick every evening just before dusk.

People wandering down the dark street saw Franklin's light a long way off. They found its glow not only friendly and beautiful, but helpful as well. Before long, other neighbours began placing similar lights in front of their own homes. Soon, the entire city was dotted with lights and everyone awoke to the value of street lighting. The matter was taken up with interest and enthusiasm as a city-wide, city-sponsored endeavour.

Just as Franklin's lantern brought guidance, safety, beauty and comfort to his city, our actions as parents light the path for our children. The guidance, kind words and correction we give show our children the way to go. Even in a darkened world, our lights can shine brightly and guide our children on the right path.

Guilt

If we confess our sins to him, he is faithful and just to forgive us and to cleanse us from every wrong.

1 John 1:9 NLT

For I will be merciful toward their iniquities, and I will remember their sins no more.

Hebrews 8:12 RSV

They sinned and rebelled against me, but I will forgive them and take away their guilt.

Jeremiah 33:8 CEV

Your iniquity is taken away, And your sin purged.

Isaiah 6:7 NKJV

Guilt

Found: Black Derby

In the 1890s a man drove by the farm of Mrs John R. McDonald. A sudden gust of wind caught his black derby hat and whirled it onto the McDonald property. He searched in vain for the hat and finally drove off bareheaded.

Mrs McDonald retrieved the hat, and for the next forty-five years various members of her family wore it. Finally the old derby was completely worn-out, beyond repair. At long last, Mrs McDonald went to the local newspaper and advertised for the owner of the hat. She noted in her ad that while the hat had been on the heads of the menfolk in her family, it had been on her conscience!

Is something nagging your heart today – an awareness that you have committed a wrong against another person, or a feeling that something has gone amiss in a relationship? Don't ignore those feelings. Seek to make amends.

A guilty conscience is a very heavy load to carry through life. Jesus died on the cross so you wouldn't have to bear that burden. He did His part; now you do yours. By His grace, obtain and maintain the freedom and peace He purchased for you by making things right.

Guilt

For the LORD your God is gracious and compassionate, and will not turn His face away from you if you return to Him.

2 Chronicles 30:9 NASB

He has removed our rebellious acts as far away from us as the east is from the west.

Psalm 103:12 NLT

I write to you, little children, Because your sins are forgiven you for His name's sake.

1 John 2:12 NKJV

You are not lacking in any spiritual gift, as you wait for the revealing of our Lord Jesus Christ; who will sustain you to the end, guiltless in the day of our Lord Jesus Christ.

1 Corinthians 1:7–8 RSV

Guilt

He Doesn't Remember

A much-loved minister of God once carried a secret burden of long-past sin buried deep in his heart. He had committed the sin many years before, during his Bible school training. No one knew what he had done, but they did know he had repented. Even so, he had suffered years of remorse over the incident without any sense of God's forgiveness.

A woman in his church deeply loved God and claimed to have visions in which Jesus Christ spoke to her. The minister, sceptical of her claims, asked her, 'The next time you speak to the Lord, would you please ask Him what sin your minister committed while he was in Bible school.' The woman agreed.

When she came to the church a few days later the minister asked, 'Did He visit you?' She said, 'Yes.'

'And did you ask Him what sin I committed?'

'Yes, I asked Him,' she replied.

'Well, what did He say?'

'He said, "I don't remember." '

The forgiveness we receive in Christ is complete. As far as God is concerned, our sin is over with and forgotten. We must learn to rest in His forgiveness and release the guilt and shame of our sin, so that we may walk in God's rest and peace.

Happiness

To the man who pleases him God gives wisdom
and knowledge and joy.

Ecclesiastes 2:26 RSV

A cheerful heart brings a smile to your face; a
sad heart makes it hard to get through the day.

Proverbs 15:13 The Message

Happiness or sadness or wealth should not keep
anyone from doing God's work.

1 Corinthians 7:30 NLT

Blessed is the man who finds wisdom, the man
who gains understanding.

Proverbs 3:13 NIV

Happiness

The Happiest People on Earth

A newspaper in England once asked this question of its readers, 'Who are the happiest people on the earth?'

The four prize-winning answers were:

A little child building sand castles.

A craftsman or artist whistling over a job well done.

A mother bathing her baby after a busy day.

A doctor who has finished a difficult and dangerous operation that saved a human life.

The paper's editors were surprised to find virtually no one submitted kings, emperors, millionaires or others of wealth and rank as the happiest people on earth.

W. Beran Wolfe once said, 'If you observe a really happy man you will find him building a boat, writing a symphony, educating his son, growing double dahlias in his garden, or looking for dinosaur eggs in the Gobi desert. He will not be searching for happiness as if it were a collar button that has rolled under the radiator. He will not be striving for it as a goal in itself. He will have become aware that he is happy in the course of living life twenty-four crowded hours of the day.'

When we shift our focus from finding happiness to seeking God and His wisdom happiness finds us.

Happiness

Is any one among you suffering? Let him pray.
Is any cheerful? Let him sing praise.

James 5:13 RSV

I will bless the LORD at all times; His praise shall
continually be in my mouth.

Psalm 34:1 NKJV

Rejoice in the Lord always. I will say it again:
Rejoice!

Philippians 4:4 NIV

Behold, we call those happy who were steadfast.
You have heard of the steadfastness of Job, and
you have seen the purpose of the Lord, how the
Lord is compassionate and merciful.

James 5:11 RSV

Happiness

The World Won't Make You Happy

When the great golfer Babe Didrikson Zaharias was dying of cancer, her husband, George Zaharias, came to her bedside. Although he desired to be strong for her sake, he found he was unable to control his emotions and began to cry. Babe said to him gently, 'Now honey, don't take on so. While I've been in the hospital, I have learned one thing. A moment of happiness is a lifetime, and I have had a lot of happiness.'

Happiness does not come wrapped in brightly coloured packages as a 'gift' given to us by others. Happiness comes when we uncover the gifts that lie within us and begin to use them to please God and bless others.

Happiness flows from within. It is found in the moments of life we label as 'quality' rather than quantity. George Bernard Shaw once said, 'This is the true joy in life: Being used for a purpose recognized by yourself as a mighty one ... Being a force of nature instead of a feverish, selfish, little clod of ailments and grievances, complaining that the world will not devote itself to making you happy.'

The only person who can truly make you happy is yourself. You simply have to decide to be.

Health & Healing

Praise the LORD, I tell myself, and never forget the good things he does for me. He forgives all my sins and heals all my diseases.

Psalm 103:2–3 NLT

He was wounded for our transgressions, He was bruised for our iniquities; The chastisement for our peace was upon Him, And by His stripes we are healed.

Isaiah 53:5 NKJV

Worship the LORD your God, and his blessing will be on your food and water. I will take away sickness from among you . . .

Exodus 23:25 NIV

And all the crowd sought to touch him, for power came forth from him and healed them all.

Luke 6:19 RSV

Health & Healing

A Healthy Dose of Words

It takes just as much energy to say a positive word as it does a negative one. In fact, it may actually take less. Research has shown that when we speak positive words – even in difficult circumstances or troubling situations – we become relaxed. As we relax, the flow of blood to the brain increases. A well-oxygenated brain can think more creatively, make wise decisions, find reasonable solutions and generate pertinent answers.

Positive words ease relationships and create an atmosphere of peace that is conducive to rest, relaxation and rejuvenation – all of which are necessary for good health.

A continual flow of negative words causes relationships to suffer, which creates an atmosphere of disharmony and makes for fitful sleep and frayed nerves – none of which are healthy!

Negative thoughts and words keep the body in a state of tension, constricting muscles and blood vessels, which often causes irrational and uncharacteristic behaviour.

God desires us to walk in the health He has provided for us in the death, burial and resurrection of Jesus. One of the ways we can do that is to watch what we say. And in order to watch what we say, we must watch what we think. Push away negative thoughts and think positive!

Health & Healing

Jesus went throughout Galilee, teaching in their synagogues, preaching the good news of the kingdom, and healing every disease and sickness among the people.

Matthew 4:23 NIV

Suddenly, a man with leprosy approached Jesus. He knelt before him, worshiping. 'Lord,' the man said, 'if you want to, you can make me well again.' Jesus touched him. 'I want to,' he said. 'Be healed!' And instantly the leprosy disappeared.

Matthew 8:2–3 NLT

The prayer of faith will save the sick, and the Lord will raise him up. And if he has committed sins, he will be forgiven.

James 5:15 NKJV

Heal the sick, raise the dead, cleanse lepers, cast out demons.

Matthew 10:8 RSV

Health & Healing

Lord, Be My Strength

Dr A. B. Simpson, a New York preacher, was plagued by poor health. Two nervous breakdowns and a heart condition led a well-known New York physician to tell him – at the age of thirty-eight – that he would never live to be forty.

In desperation, Simpson went to the Bible to find out what Jesus had to say about disease. He became convinced that Jesus always meant for healing to be a part of redemption. He asked Christ to enter him and to become his physical strength until his life's work was accomplished. He later said, 'Every fibre in me was tingling with the sense of God's presence.'

Days later, Simpson climbed a 3,000-foot mountain. He said, 'When I reached the top, the world of weakness and fear was lying at my feet. From that time on I literally had a new heart.' He went on to preach 3,000 sermons in the next three years, holding as many as twenty meetings a week. He amassed an amazing volume of work before he died – at the age of seventy-six.

Whatever you may be facing that leaves you feeling weak and fearful, God will take your weakness and replace it with His strength and bring healing to your life.

Hope

Behold, the eye of the LORD is upon them that
fear him, upon them that hope in his mercy.

Psalm 33:18 KJV

It is good that one should hope and wait quietly
For the salvation of the LORD.

Lamentations 3:26 NKJV

Happy is he whose help is the God of Jacob,
whose hope is in the LORD his God.

Psalm 146:5 RSV

Christ has also introduced us to God's unde-
served kindness on which we take our stand. So
we are happy, as we look forward to sharing in
the glory of God.

Romans 5:2 CEV

Hope

Perfect Timing

Carolyn, a preacher's wife, had just found evidence that her daughter was involved in questionable activities. Because of her position, however, Carolyn felt that to tell anyone might expose her husband and his ministry to ridicule. To keep the secret was painful – she needed a friend. In near desperation, she cried out to God, 'I've got to talk to *someone*! Can't You send me somebody I can trust?'

Almost before she had finished praying, the doorbell rang. When she opened the door, there stood another preacher's wife. She was new to the city and had come to introduce herself.

Carolyn soon discovered her newfound friend had also gone through the struggle of raising a rebellious teenager. When Carolyn poured out her problem to her new friend, the friend offered to pray for her. Within minutes, Carolyn felt a profound peace fill her heart. She realized God had sent her help the very *minute* she needed it. In that, she felt confident she could trust Him to begin a healing in her daughter's heart, and in her own heart, just as quickly!

Hope in God is never misplaced. He always comes through. The very minute we pray, the answer is sent – and sometimes it arrives before we even finish.

Hope

Praise be to the God and Father of our Lord
Jesus Christ! In his great mercy he has given us
new birth into a living hope through the resurrection of Jesus Christ from the dead, and into
an inheritance that can never perish, spoil or
fade – kept in heaven for you.

1 Peter 1:3–4 NIV

O LORD, you alone are my hope. I've trusted
you, O LORD, from childhood.

Psalm 71:5 NLT

When they see me waiting, expecting your
Word, those who fear you will take heart and
be glad.

Psalm 119:74 The Message

Hope in God and wait expectantly for Him, for
I shall yet praise Him, my Help and my God.

Psalm 42:5 AMP

Hope

God Is Real

Dr Walter Eerdman wrote a best-seller some years ago entitled *Source of Power in Famous Lives*. In it, he gave biographical sketches of fifty great men and women of history – among them David Livingstone, Jenny Lind, Clara Barton, Frances Willard, Christopher Columbus and Oliver Cromwell.

Eerdman drew this conclusion about the people he had profiled: 'In their lives, God was a reality.'

Truly great people share a common source of power – they simply apply that power in different ways. Some have greater public success and thus attain to a greater degree of fame and prominence than others. Many less famous people, however, have also encouraged others with their stories of personal triumphs and victories. This shows that the power that comes from having a real relationship with God isn't limited to the rich and famous. It can be attained by anyone, regardless of his or her wealth or position in society.

Genuine power from God is manifest as hope in times of disaster, calm in times of crises, direction in times of confusion, and an enduring faith in times of fear. Anyone can know this power if they will put their hope in God and allow Him to become a reality in their lives.

Hospitality

In all things I have shown you that by so toiling one must help the weak, remembering the words of the Lord Jesus, how he said, 'It is more blessed to give than to receive.'

Acts 20:35 RSV

When God's children are in need, be the one to help them out. And get into the habit of inviting guests home for dinner or, if they need lodging, for the night.

Romans 12:13 NLT

Be hospitable to one another without grumbling.

1 Peter 4:9 NKJV

Dear children, let us not love with words or tongue but with actions and in truth.

1 John 3:18 NIV

Hospitality

Home Sweet Home

In *Secret Strength*, Joni Eareckson Tada writes a wonderful tribute to a genuine 'home, sweet home':

'Not long ago I entered a friend's home and immediately sensed the glory of God. No, that impression was not based on some heebie-jeebie feeling or super-spiritual instinct. And it had nothing to do with several Christian plaques I spotted hanging in the hallway. Yet there was a peace and orderliness that pervaded that home. Joy and music hung in the air. Although the kids were normal, active youngsters, everyone's activity seemed to dovetail together, creating the impression that the home had direction, that the kids really cared about each other, that the parents put love into action.

'We didn't even spend that much time "fellowshipping" in the usual sense of the word – talking about the Bible or praying together. Yet we laughed. And really heard each other. And opened our hearts like family members. After dinner I left that home refreshed. It was a place where God's essential being was on display. His kindness, His love, His justice. It was filled with God's glory.'

Real hospitality is more than pretty dishes and fancy centrepieces. It is inviting God's presence into our home and then sharing His peace and love with others.

Hospitality

Cheerfully share your home with those who
need a meal or a place to stay.

1 Peter 4:9 NLT

I tell you the truth, anyone who gives you a cup
of water in my name because you belong to
Christ will certainly not lose his reward.

Mark 9:41 NIV

Be sure to welcome strangers into your home.
By doing this, some people have welcomed
angels as guests, without even knowing it.

Hebrews 13:2 CEV

It's good work you're doing, helping these trav-
ellers on their way, hospitality worthy of God
himself!

3 John 8 The Message

Hospitality

'Guess Who's Coming for Dinner'

A businessman called his wife one day to get her permission to bring home to dinner a visiting foreigner. At the time, the wife had three children in school and one toddler at home, so she had a full workload on any given day, apart from entertaining strangers. Still, she consented and the meal she prepared was both delicious and graciously served. The visitor, an important official in Spain, had a delightful time and thanked the couple repeatedly for inviting him into their home and treating him to a home-cooked meal and an evening of fellowship.

Years later, friends of this family went to Spain as missionaries. Their work was brought to a standstill, however, by government regulations. This particular Spanish official got word that the missionaries were friends of the couple who had hosted him in such a loving manner, and he used his influence to clear away the restrictions on their behalf. A church exists today in that province of Spain, due in part to the setting of one extra place at one dinner table!

As busy as you may be today, take time for the people God may bring across your path. Who knows what plan God may have for both of your futures.

Jealousy

For where you have envy and selfish ambition,
there you find disorder and every evil practice.

James 3:16 NIV

If we live by the Spirit, let us also walk by the
Spirit. Let us have no self-conceit, no provoking
of one another, no envy of one another.

Galatians 5:25–26 RSV

You shall not covet.

Exodus 20:17 NKJV

Wrath is fierce and anger is a flood, But who
can stand before jealousy?

Proverbs 27:4 NASB

Jealousy

Focus on What You Have

Former *Good Morning America* co-host Joan Lunden recalls, 'When I first came on [the] program in 1978, hosting with David Hartman, he got to interview all the celebrities and politicians and kings. I got the information spots. . . . I received piles of letters from women who were unhappy that I was allowing myself to be used in this way. Well, the fact was I enjoyed those spots and I was good at them. I had to accept that it was either that way or no way at all.

'I can't see any reason to spend your time frustrated, angry, or upset about things you don't have or you can't have or you can't yet do. I drill this into my children when I hear them say, "I don't have this." I'll say, "Don't focus on what you don't have. Focus on what you do have and be grateful for it. Be proud of what you can do. Those things you can't do yet, maybe you will do." '

When we envy others who have gifts and talents that we don't, we get nowhere. God never asks us to become something that we aren't, all He asks is that we use the gifts He's given us to the best of our ability.

Jealousy

Do not envy wicked men, do not desire their company; for their hearts plot violence, and their lips talk about making trouble.

Proverbs 24:1–2 NIV

But if your heart is full of bitter jealousy and selfishness, don't brag or lie to cover up the truth.

James 3:14 CEV

Do you think that the Scripture says in vain, 'The Spirit who dwells in us yearns jealously?'

James 4:5 NKJV

The LORD your God is a consuming fire, a jealous God.

Deuteronomy 4:24 AMP

Jealousy

Envy Devours

Few people have undergone the trials and tribulations of Alexander Solzhenitsyn, who suffered decades of horrendous hardship as a political exile in the Siberian prison system known as the 'gulag'. We can learn from Solzhenitsyn not only because he is a survivor, but because he has been in a situation that few of us have ever known – an existence of near total deprivation. He has not only lived without luxuries, but without necessities.

He writes as few can in *The Prison Chronicle:*

'Don't be afraid of misfortune and do not yearn after happiness. It is, after all, all the same. The bitter doesn't last forever, and the sweet never fills the cup to overflowing. It is enough if you don't freeze in the cold and if hunger and thirst don't claw at your sides. If your back isn't broken, if your feet can walk, if both arms work, if both eyes can see, and if both ears can hear, then whom should you envy? And why? Our envy of others devours us most of all. Rub your eyes and purify your heart and prize above all else in the world those who love you and wish you well.'

Joy

You shall go out in joy, and be led forth in peace; the mountains and the hills before you shall break forth into singing, and all the trees of the field shall clap their hands.

Isaiah 55:12 RSV

Now those you have rescued will return to Jerusalem, singing on their way. They will be crowned with great happiness, never again to be burdened with sadness and sorrow.

Isaiah 51:11 CEV

'Go and celebrate ... This is a sacred day before our Lord. Don't be dejected and sad, for the joy of the LORD is your strength.'

Nehemiah 8:10 NLT

What's more, our hearts brim with joy since we've taken for our own his holy name.

Psalm 33:21 The Message

Joy

Show Me How to Live

Joni Eareckson Tada lives such an inspirational life of ministry today, it is often difficult for others to accept the fact that in the wake of her paralysing accident, Joni experienced nearly three years of depression and suicidal despair. She finally reached the point where she prayed, 'God, if I can't die, show me how to live, please!'

Things didn't change for Joni overnight, but they did begin to change. Very little about her *situation* changed, but her outlook – her attitude, her mind, her perspective, her spirit – began to change and grow. She knew with an increasing assurance that God would help her learn how to do what seemed to be impossible: handle life in a wheelchair.

Are you facing a seemingly impossible situation today? Do you feel as if any option you might have is really no option at all? Perhaps it's time to pray: 'God, show me how to live in the midst of this situation.' Accepting God's help in coping with the despair and hopelessness of a situation is very often the first step God uses in preparing us to live a new way – a way that is far beyond mere coping. His way is always one of true fulfilment and joy.

Joy

My soul is satisfied as with a rich feast, and my mouth praises you with joyful lips when I think of you on my bed, and meditate on you in the watches of the night.

Psalm 63:5–6 NRSV

You have given me greater joy than those who have abundant harvests of grain and wine.

Psalm 4:7 NLT

We cried as we went out to plant our seeds. Now let us celebrate as we bring in the crops. We cried on the way to plant our seeds, but we will celebrate and shout as we bring in the crops.

Psalm 126:5–6 CEV

Now is your time of grief, but I will see you again and you will rejoice, and no-one will take away your joy.

John 16:22 NIV

Joy

Overflowing Joy

One day during her morning devotions, Jeannie found herself weeping as she read Psalm 139:23, 'Search me, O God, and know my heart'. She cried out to the Lord to cleanse her of several bad attitudes she had been harbouring. Later that morning as she boarded an aeroplane, she had a strong feeling that God was confirming to her that He had forgiven her and could now use her for a special assignment. She whispered a prayer. 'Lord, help me to stay awake.'

Jeannie usually took travel sickness pills before flying, and therefore, often slept from take-off to landing. On this flight, however, she forced herself to stay awake. A woman took the seat next to her on the flight and as they began to talk, the woman asked, 'Why do you have so much joy?' Jeannie replied, 'Because of Jesus.' And for the next three hours, she had a wonderful opportunity to witness to the woman. Later, she sent her a Bible and they exchanged letters. Then late one evening, the woman called and Jeannie led her to the Lord over the phone.

The Lord will not only hear your heart's cry today, but His answer will fill you with overflowing joy that you will be able to share with others.

Justice

As for the Almighty, we cannot find Him; He is excellent in power, In judgment and abundant justice; He does not oppress.

Job 37:23 NKJV

Rise up, O LORD, in your anger; lift yourself up against the fury of my enemies; awake, O my God; you have appointed a judgment.

Psalm 7:6 NRSV

'Let him who boasts boast about this: that he understands and knows me, that I am the LORD, who exercises kindness, justice and righteousness on earth, for in these I delight,' declares the LORD.

Jeremiah 9:24 NIV

'He will not crush those who are weak, or quench the smallest hope, until he brings full justice with his final victory. And his name will be the hope of all the world.'

Matthew 12:20–21 NLT

Justice

Divine Justice

On their way back from a meeting of the Greek Orthodox Archdiocese, Father Demetrios Frangos and Father Germanos Stavropoulos were in a car accident. A young woman, high on drugs, drove into their car while they waited at the traffic lights. Both priests were killed instantly. The woman, a legal secretary with a seven-year-old daughter, had no previous police record, but admitted to having used drugs for ten years. She was charged with murder and several other felonies. The tabloid headlines were especially vicious, referring to her as the 'priest killer'.

Father Demetrios' son, George, responded with forgiveness, not anger. He offered to help provide the woman with a lawyer and hoped if she was convicted the sentence would be short. He said, 'The last thing my father would have wanted was to make an example [of her]. This woman is anguished and troubled to begin with ... we have to look after the innocent one, the child. It is extremely important that her child be told that we forgive her mother.'

George Frangos loved his father and grieved for him, but more important to him than 'legal justice' was 'divine justice' – that this woman and her little daughter know the love of Jesus Christ.

Justice

God presented him as a sacrifice of atonement, through faith in his blood. He did this to demonstrate his justice, because in his forbearance he had left the sins committed beforehand unpunished.

Romans 3:25 NIV

The LORD has made himself known, he has executed judgment; the wicked are snared in the work of their own hands.

Psalm 9:16 RSV

Let true justice prevail, so you may live and occupy the land that the LORD your God is giving you.

Deuteronomy 16:20 NLT

The King is mighty, he loves justice – you have established equity; in Jacob you have done what is just and right.

Psalm 99:4 NIV

Justice

Justice and Mercy

One of New York City's most popular mayors was Fiorello LaGuardia. Nearly every older New Yorker has a favourite memory of him. Some recall the day he read the funny papers over the radio, with all the appropriate inflections, because a strike had kept the Sunday newspapers off the stands.

Once, the mayor chose to preside in a night court. An old woman was brought before him on that bitterly cold night. The charge was stealing a loaf of bread. She explained that her family was starving. LaGuardia replied, 'I've got to punish you. The law makes no exception. I must fine you ten dollars.' At that, he reached into his own pocket and pulled out a ten-dollar bill. 'Well,' he said, 'here's the ten dollars to pay your fine, which I now remit.' He then tossed the ten-dollar bill into his own hat and declared, 'I'm going to fine everybody in this courtroom fifty cents for living in a town where a person has to steal bread in order to eat. Mr Bailiff, collect the fines and give them to this defendant.'

After the hat was passed, the incredulous old woman left the courtroom with a new light in her eyes and $47.50 in her pocket to buy groceries! That's God's kind of justice!

Loneliness

Behold, I am with you and will keep you wherever you go, and will bring you back to this land; for I will not leave you until I have done that of which I have spoken to you.

Genesis 28:15 RSV

Those who know your name trust in you, for you, O LORD, have never abandoned anyone who searches for you.

Psalm 9:10 NLT

God assured us, 'I'll never let you down, never walk off and leave you.'

Hebrews 13:5 The Message

God sets the lonely in families, he leads forth the prisoners with singing.

Psalm 68:6 NIV

Loneliness

Being Rooted

The next time you visit a very dense forest, try to imagine what is taking place under your feet. Scientists now know when the roots of trees come into contact with one another, a substance is released which encourages the growth of a particular kind of fungus. This fungus helps link roots of different trees – even those of dissimilar species. If one tree has access to water, another to nutrients and a third to sunlight, the fungus enables the transfer of these items to trees that may be in need. Thus, the trees have the means of sharing with one another to preserve them all.

Our culture today applauds individualism. However, it tends to isolate people from one another and cut them off from the mainstream of life. With more and more people working at home or in walled offices and with schedules crammed tighter than ever with work and activities, feelings of loneliness are more likely to increase than decrease. Don't allow isolation to overcome you!

Reach out to others. Begin to give where you can. Learn to receive when others give to you. Build a network of friends, not just colleagues. And above all, root yourself into a group that nourishes and builds you up spiritually – your church.

Loneliness

Height nor depth, nor any other created thing, shall be able to separate us from the love of God which is in Christ Jesus our Lord.

Romans 8:39 NKJV

The eternal God is thy refuge, and underneath are the everlasting arms.

Deuteronomy 33:27 KJV

Be still, and know that I am God; I will be exalted among the nations, I will be exalted in the earth.

Psalm 46:10 NIV

For you are my hiding place; you protect me from trouble. You surround me with songs of victory.

Psalm 32:7 NLT

Loneliness

Don't Go It Alone

A woman was in a serious car accident in a city far from home. She felt so enclosed in a cocoon of pain, she didn't realize how lonely she was until a 'forgotten' friend in the city came to visit her. She firmly, but gently said to her, 'You should not be alone.'

In the weeks that followed, this friend's advice rang in the injured woman's ears and helped her to overcome her otherwise reserved nature. When another friend called from a city several hundred miles away to say she wanted to come to stay with her, the injured woman didn't say, 'Don't bother' – as would have been her normal response. Instead, she said, 'Please come.' The friend was a wonderful encouragement to her. Then, yet another friend offered to come and help in her recovery. Again she swallowed her pride and said, 'Please do.' This friend stayed for several months until the injured woman was able to care for herself.

Even Jesus did not carry His own cross all the way to Calvary. He allowed another to help shoulder His burden. It's all right to ask for help and to receive help. You don't have to 'go it alone'. Let a friend help you!

Loss

And God will wipe away every tear from their eyes; there shall be no more death, nor sorrow, nor crying. There shall be no more pain.

Revelation 21:4 NKJV

Weeping may remain for a night, but rejoicing comes in the morning.

Psalm 30:5 NIV

He heals the heartbroken and bandages their wounds.

Psalm 147:3 The Message

Everything on earth has its own time and its own season ... For crying and laughing, weeping and dancing.

Ecclesiastes 3:1,4 CEV

Loss

God Grieves with You

In *Women Who Do Too Much,* Patricia Sprinkle writes: 'Three months before I spoke with Nancy, her husband lost a four-year battle to a degenerative brain disease. She said, "This was a brilliant man, a gentle man, a man with a terrific sense of humor. I grieved as he lost his ability to walk, pick up things from the floor, write, speak clearly. We had been married for thirty years and expected to grow old together. Suddenly, in one day, our life changed. He flew to Mayo Clinic one morning and called me that night with the doctor's diagnosis. They could do nothing for him.

' "I remember thinking after I hung up the phone, life is never going to be the same again. Nobody gets a rehearsal for this. You don't get to practice.

' "I was furious with God – banged my fist on many tables. But I learned to thank God that God is God. God didn't get bowled over by my fury. Instead, He told me, 'I won't leave you. I'm as sad about this as you are. I grieve with you.' The shared grief of God gets me through my own." '

Jesus called the Holy Spirit the 'Comforter'. He is with us every moment of our lives.

Loss

To all who mourn in Israel, he will give beauty
for ashes, joy instead of mourning, praise
instead of despair.

Isaiah 61:3 NLT

Blessed are those who mourn, for they will be
comforted.

Matthew 5:4 NIV

For as the sufferings of Christ abound in us, so
our consolation also abounds through Christ.

2 Corinthians 1:5 NKJV

Laugh with your happy friends when they're
happy; share tears when they're down.

Romans 12:15 The Message

Loss

Trust in Jesus

As Louisa Stead, her husband and their young daughter were enjoying an oceanside picnic one day, they noticed a young boy struggling in the surf. As the drowning boy cried out for help, Mr Stead rushed to save him. Unfortunately, the terrified boy pulled him under the waves and both drowned as Louisa and her daughter watched helplessly from the shore.

In the sorrowful days that followed, the grief-stricken widow began to put pen to paper and the result was a hymn now known to millions:

'Tis so sweet to trust in Jesus, just to take Him at His word, just to rest upon His promise, just to know, 'Thus saith the Lord.'
O how sweet to trust in Jesus, just to trust His cleansing blood, just in simple faith to plunge me 'neath the healing, cleansing flood!
Yes, 'tis sweet to trust in Jesus, just from sin and self to cease, just from Jesus simply taking life and rest and joy and peace.
I'm so glad I learned to trust Thee, Precious Jesus, Saviour, Friend; and I know that Thou art with me, wilt be with me to the end.

In the midst of our pain and grief, Jesus is right there with us.

Love

Now these three remain: faith, hope and love.
But the greatest of these is love.

1 Corinthians 13:13 NIV

Pursue a godly life, along with faith, love, perseverance, and gentleness.

1 Timothy 6:11 NLT

Above all things have fervent love for one another, for 'love will cover a multitude of sins.'

1 Peter 4:8 NKJV

Above all these put on love, which binds everything together in perfect harmony.

Colossians 3:14 RSV

Love

Jesus Loves Me

A woman minister received a call from a friend she had not seen in two years. The friend said, 'My husband is leaving me for another woman. I need for you to pray with me.' The minister said, 'Come quickly.'

When her friend arrived, the minister could not help but notice that her friend was carelessly dressed, had gained weight, and had not combed her hair or put on make-up. As they began to talk, the friend admitted to being an uninteresting, nagging wife and a sloppy housekeeper. The minister quickly concluded to herself, *My friend has grown to hate herself!*

When her friend paused to ask for her advice, the minister said only, 'Will you join me in a song?' Surprised, her friend agreed. The minister began to sing, 'Jesus loves me, this I know.' Her friend joined in, tears flooding her eyes. 'If Jesus loves me, I must love myself, too,' she concluded.

Amazing changes followed. Because she felt loved and loveable, this woman was transformed into the confident woman she once had been. In the process, she recaptured her husband's heart.

We can never accept God's love beyond the degree to which we are willing to love ourselves. Our part is to believe, to receive and to give.

Love

Love your neighbor as yourself: I am the LORD.
Leviticus 19:18 NKJV

For the whole law can be summed up in this
one command: 'Love your neighbor as yourself.'
Galatians 5:14 NLT

By this all men will know that you are my disciples, if you have love for one another.
John 13:35 RSV

My beloved friends, let us continue to love each
other since love comes from God. Everyone
who loves is born of God and experiences a relationship with God.
1 John 4:7–8 The Message

Love

For Love

Perhaps the most famous 'mother' in the world is the late Mother Teresa. In 1948 as Sister Teresa, she was given permission to leave her order of nearly twenty years and travel to India. On her first day in Calcutta, Teresa picked up five abandoned children and brought them to her 'school'. Before the year ended, she had forty-one students learning about hygiene in her classroom in a public park. Shortly afterwards, a new congregation was approved. Mother Teresa quickly named it 'Missionaries of Charity'. Within two years, their attention had become focused on the care of the dying.

Once, a poor beggar was picked up as he was dying in a pile of rubbish. Reduced by suffering and hunger to a mere spectre, Mother Teresa took him to the Home for the Dying and put him in bed. When she began to wash him, she discovered his body was covered with worms. Pieces of skin came off as she washed him. For a brief moment, the man revived. In his semi-conscious state, he asked, 'Why do you do it?'

'For love.'

Ask any mother why she does what she does and you are likely to receive the same answer. Love is both a mother's work – and a mother's reward.

Marriage

And the LORD God said, 'It is not good that man should be alone; I will make him a helper comparable to him.

Genesis 2:18 NKJV

Therefore what God has joined together, let man not separate.

Matthew 19:6 NIV

He who finds a wife finds a good thing, And obtains favor from the LORD.

Proverbs 18:22 NKJV

Honor marriage, and guard the sacredness of sexual intimacy between wife and husband. God draws a firm line against casual and illicit sex.

Hebrews 13:4 The Message

Marriage

Conquer Conflict

Two men once made small talk at a party: 'You and your wife seem to get along very well,' one man said. 'Don't you ever have differences?' 'Sure,' said the other. 'We often have differences, but we get over them quickly.'

'How do you do that?' the first man asked. 'Simple,' said the second. 'I don't tell her we have them.'

In *Letters to Philip,* Charles Shedd describes a slightly different situation – harmony that comes after love has conquered conflict. He writes: 'In one town where I lived two rivers met. There was a bluff high above them where you could sit and watch their coming together . . . Those two nice streams came at each other like fury. They clashed in a wild commotion of frenzy and confusion . . . Then, as you watched, you could almost see the angry whitecaps pair off, bow in respect to each other, and join forces as if to say, "Let us get along now. Ahead of us there is something better." '

Don't avoid the conflicts in your marriage. Choose to apply God's love in order to overcome them. Unresolved conflicts weaken a marriage, but conflicts resolved with love help make two small streams into one large river, flowing on to something better.

Marriage

Therefore a man leaves his father and his mother and cleaves to his wife, and they become one flesh.

Genesis 2:24 RSV

For the husband is the head of the wife as Christ is the head of the church, his body, of which he is the Saviour.

Ephesians 5:23 NIV

You wives must accept the authority of your husbands, even those who refuse to accept the Good News. Your godly lives will speak to them better than any words. They will be won over by watching your pure, godly behavior.

1 Peter 3:1–2 NLT

A wife must put her husband first. This is her duty as a follower of the Lord. A husband must love his wife and not abuse her.

Colossians 3:18–19 CEV

Marriage

Kill Her with Kindness

After two years of marriage, Pete no longer saw his wife as interesting, fun or attractive. In his mind, he regarded her as an overweight, sloppy housekeeper, with a faultfinding personality. He visited a divorce solicitor, who advised him: 'Pete, if you really want to get even with your wife, start treating her like a queen! Do everything in your power to serve her, please her and make her feel special. Then, after a couple of months of this royal treatment, pack your bags and leave. That way you'll disappoint her as much as she has disappointed you.'

Pete could hardly wait to enact the plan! He picked up a dozen roses on his way home, helped his wife with the dishes, brought her breakfast in bed, and began complimenting her on her clothes, cooking, and housekeeping. He even treated her to a weekend away.

After three months, the solicitor called and said, 'Well, I have the divorce papers ready for you to sign. In a matter of minutes, you can be a happy bachelor.'

'Are you crazy?' Pete said. 'My wife has made so many changes. I wouldn't think of divorcing her now!'

Kindness extended towards another person may or may not change that person, but it certainly changes the perspective of the kindness-giver!

Mercy

Let us therefore come boldly to the throne of grace, that we may obtain mercy and find grace to help in time of need.

Hebrews 4:16 NKJV

The LORD answered: All right. I am the LORD, and I show mercy and kindness to anyone I choose.

Exodus 33:19 CEV

Give knowledge of salvation to his people in the forgiveness of their sins, through the tender mercy of our God.

Luke 1:77–78 RSV

God is all mercy and grace – not quick to anger, is rich in love. God is good to one and all; everything he does is suffused with grace.

Psalm 145:8–9 The Message

Mercy

In Need of Mercy

According to a traditional Hebrew legend, Abraham was sitting by his tent one evening when he saw an old man walking towards him. He could tell long before the man arrived that he was weary from age and travel. Abraham rushed out to greet him and then invited him into his tent. He washed the old man's feet and gave him something to drink and eat.

The old man immediately began eating without saying a prayer or invoking a blessing. Abraham asked him, 'Don't you worship God?' The old traveller replied, 'I worship fire only and reverence no other god.' Upon hearing this, Abraham grabbed the old man by the shoulders and with indignation, threw him out of his tent into the cold night air.

The old man walked off into the night and after he had gone, God called to His friend Abraham and asked where the stranger was. Abraham replied, 'I forced him out of my tent because he did not worship You.' The Lord responded, 'I have suffered him these eighty years although he dishonours Me. Could you not endure him one night?'

Do you know someone who needs to experience your mercy as a tangible expression of the mercy God is extending to her?

Mercy

Who is a God like you, who pardons sin and forgives the transgression of the remnant of his inheritance? You do not stay angry for ever but delight to show mercy.

Micah 7:18 NIV

For you, O LORD, are good and forgiving; abounding in steadfast love to all who call on you.

Psalm 86:5 NRSV

The LORD still waits for you to come to him so he can show you his love and compassion. For the LORD is a faithful God. Blessed are those who wait for him to help them.

Isaiah 30:18 NLT

The LORD is always kind to those who worship him, and he keeps his promises to their descendants who faithfully obey him.

Psalm 103:17–18 CEV

Mercy

God's Mercy

When William Gladstone was Chancellor of the Exchequer, he once requested that the Treasury send him certain statistics upon which he might base his budget proposals. The statistician made a mistake. But Gladstone was so certain of this man's concern for accuracy that he didn't take the time to verify the figures. As a result, he went before the House of Commons and made a speech based upon the incorrect figures given to him. His speech was no sooner published than the inaccuracies were exposed, and Gladstone became the brunt of public ridicule.

The Chancellor sent for the statistician who had given him the wrong information. The man arrived full of fear and shame, certain he was going to be sacked. Instead, Gladstone said, 'I know how much you must be disturbed over what has happened, and I have sent for you to put you at your ease. For a long time you have been engaged in handling the intricacies of the national accounts, and this is the first mistake that you have made. I want to congratulate you, and express to you my keen appreciation.'

God constantly extends His mercy to you. Are there times when your child is in need of this kind of mercy?

Obedience

To obey is better than sacrifice, and to heed than the fat of rams.

1 Samuel 15:22 NRSV

Listen closely, Israel, to everything I say. Be careful to obey. Then all will go well with you, and you will have many children in the land flowing with milk and honey, just as the LORD, the God of your ancestors, promised you.

Deuteronomy 6:3 NLT

If they obey and serve him, they will spend the rest of their days in prosperity and their years in contentment.

Job 36:11 NIV

He who has my commandments and keeps them, he it is who loves me; and he who loves me will be loved by my Father, and I will love him and manifest myself to him.

John 14:21 RSV

Obedience

Ready Obedience

The story is told of a great military captain who, after a full day of battle, sat by the fire with several of his officers and began talking over the events of the day with them.

He asked them, 'Who did the best today on the field of battle?'

One officer told of a man who had fought very bravely all day, and then just before dusk, had been severely wounded. Another told of a man who had taken a hit for a fellow soldier, sparing his friend's life but very possibly losing his own. Yet another told of the man who had led the charge into battle.

The captain heard them out and then said, 'No, I fear you are all mistaken. The best man in the field today was the soldier who was just lifting up his arm to strike the enemy, but, upon hearing the trumpet sound the retreat, checked himself, dropped his arm without striking the blow, and retreated. That perfect and ready obedience to the will of his general is the noblest thing that was done today on the battlefield.'

God's Word tells us that obedience is better than sacrifice. God desires that we learn to obey Him and walk in His will for our lives. He will never lead us astray.

Obedience

'If you listen to these regulations and obey them
faithfully, the LORD your God will keep his
covenant of unfailing love with you, as he
solemnly promised your ancestors.'

Deuteronomy 7:12 NLT

If you keep my commands, you'll remain
intimately at home in my love. That's what I've
done – kept my Father's commands and made
myself at home in his love.

John 15:10 The Message

When we obey God, we are sure that we know
him ... We truly love God only when we obey
him as we should, and then we know that we
belong to him.

1 John 2:3,5 CEV

Dear friends, if our hearts do not condemn us,
we have confidence before God and receive
from him anything we ask, because we obey his
commands and do what pleases him.

1 John 3:21–22 NIV

Obedience

Obeying God's Call

In *Dakota*, Kathleen Norris writes: 'A
Benedictine sister from the Philippines once
told me what her community did when some
sisters took to the streets in the popular revolt
against the Marcos regime. Some did not think
it proper for nuns to demonstrate in public, let
alone risk arrest. In a group meeting that began
and ended with prayer, the sisters who wished
to continue demonstrating explained that this
was for them a religious obligation; those who
disapproved also had their say. Everyone spoke;
everyone heard and gave counsel.

'It was eventually decided that the nuns
who were demonstrating should continue to do
so; those who wished to express solidarity but
were unable to march would prepare food and
provide medical assistance to the demonstrators,
and those who disapproved would pray for
everyone. The sisters laughed and said, "If one of
the conservative sisters was praying that we
young, crazy ones would come to our senses
and stay off the streets, that was okay. We were
still a community." '

God calls some to action, others to support
and still others to pray. Each will be doing what
is 'right' in His eyes if they obey His call!

Patience

Patient endurance is what you need now, so you will continue to do God's will. Then you will receive all that he has promised.

Hebrews 10:36 NLT

Consider it a sheer gift, friends, when tests and challenges come at you from all sides. You know that under pressure, your faith-life is forced into the open and shows its true colors. So don't try to get out of anything prematurely. Let it do its work so you become mature and well-developed, not deficient in any way.

James 1:2–4 The Message

He will give eternal life to everyone who has patiently done what is good in the hope of receiving glory, honor, and life that lasts forever.

Romans 2:7 CEV

We pray this in order that you may live a life worthy of the Lord and may please him in every way . . . Being strengthened with all power according to his glorious might so that you may have great endurance and patience.

Colossians 1:10–11 NIV

Patience

What Patience Is

One of the most beautiful descriptions of patience in all of classic literature is this from Bishop Horne:

'Patience is the guardian of faith, the preserver of peace, the cherisher of love, the teacher of humility. Patience governs the flesh, strengthens the spirit, sweetens the temper, stifles anger, extinguishes envy, subdues pride; she bridles the tongue, restrains the hand, tramples upon temptations, endures persecutions, consummates martyrdom.

'Patience produces unity in the church, loyalty in the state, harmony in families and societies; she comforts the poor, and moderates the rich; she makes us humble in prosperity, cheerful in adversity, unmoved by calumny and reproach; she teaches us to forgive those who have injured us, and to be the first in asking forgiveness of those whom we have injured; she delights the faithful, and invites the unbelieving; she adorns the woman, and approves the man; she is beautiful in either sex and every age . . .

'She rides not in the whirlwind and stormy tempest of passion, but her throne is the humble and contrite heart, and her kingdom is the kingdom of peace.'

When the opportunity arises to be patient with your child, consider how God would respond to you in a similar circumstance.

Patience

Put on a heart of compassion, kindness, humility, gentleness and patience; bearing with one another, and forgiving each other, whoever has a complaint against anyone; just as the Lord forgave you, so also should you.

Colossians 3:12–13 NASB

Be humble and gentle. Be patient with each other, making allowance for each other's faults because of your love.

Ephesians 4:2 NLT

God is the one who makes us patient and cheerful. I pray that he will help you live at peace with each other, as you follow Christ.

Romans 15:5 CEV

We do not want you to become lazy, but to imitate those who through faith and patience inherit what has been promised.

Hebrews 6:12 NIV

Patience

Squeeze Please

According to a fable, a woman showed up one snowy morning at 5 am at the home of an 'examiner' of 'suitable mother' candidates. Ushered in, she was asked to sit for three hours past her appointment time before she was interviewed. The first question given to her in the interview was, 'Can you spell?' 'Yes,' she said. 'Then spell "cook".' The woman responded, 'C-O-O-K.'

The examiner then asked, 'Do you know anything about numbers?' The woman replied, 'Yes, sir, some things.' The examiner said, 'Please add two plus two.' The candidate replied, 'Four.'

'Fine,' announced the examiner. 'We'll be in touch.' At the board meeting of examiners held the next day, the examiner reported that the woman had all the qualifications to be a fine mother. He said, 'First I tested her on self-denial, making her arrive at five in the morning on a snowy day. Then I tested her on patience. She waited three hours without complaint. Third, I tested her on temper, asking her questions a child could answer. She never showed indignation or anger. She'll make a fine mother.' And all on the board agreed.

When you think you've run out of patience, remember there's always a little more toothpaste in the toothpaste tube – you just have to squeeze a little harder!

Peace

Peace I leave with you; My peace I give to you;
not as the world gives, do I give to you.

John 14:27 NASB

I will lie down and sleep in peace, for you alone,
O LORD, make me dwell in safety.

Psalm 4:8 NIV

You give peace of mind to all who love your
Law. Nothing can make them fall.

Psalm 119:165 CEV

You will keep him in perfect peace, Whose
mind is stayed on You, Because he trusts in You.

Isaiah 26:3 NKJV

Peace

Help Me!

In an article written for *America* magazine entitled, 'Praying in a Time of Depression', Jane Redmont wrote:

'On a quick trip to New York for a consulting job, a week or two into the anti-depressant drug and feeling no relief, I fell into a seven-hour anxiety attack with recurring suicidal feelings. On the morning after my arrival I found I could not focus my attention; yet focus was crucial in the job I was contracted to do for twenty-four hours, as recorder and process observer at a conference of urban activists that was beginning later that day. I felt as if I were about to jump out of my skin – or throw myself under a truck.

'An hour away from the beginning of the conference, walking uptown on a noisy Manhattan street in the afternoon, I prayed ... perhaps out loud, I am not sure. I said with all my strength, "Jesus, I don't usually ask you for much, but I am asking You now, in the name of all those people whom You healed ... *help me*."

'Within an hour, I was calm again.'

God is our high tower, a refuge in times of trouble. We can pray in the midst of anxiety and depression and God will fill us with His peace that passes understanding.

Peace

Turn your back on sin; do something good.
Embrace peace – don't let it get away!
Psalm 34:14 The Message

Therefore, since we have been made right in
God's sight by faith, we have peace with God
because of what Jesus Christ our Lord has done
for us.

Romans 5:1 NLT

May the God of hope fill you with all joy and
peace as you trust in him, so that you may over-
flow with hope by the power of the Holy Spirit.
Romans 15:13 NIV

The meek shall inherit the earth; and shall
delight themselves in the abundance of peace.
Psalm 37:11 KJV

Peace

The Wind Blows

Tom Dooley was a young doctor who gave up an easy, prosperous career in the States to organize hospitals in south-east Asia and to pour out his life in service to the afflicted people there. As he lay dying of cancer at the age of thirty-four, Dooley wrote to the president of Notre Dame, his alma mater:

'Dear Father Hesburgh: They've got me down. Flat on the back, with plaster, sand bags, and hot water bottles . . . I think of one Divine Doctor and my personal fund of grace . . . I have monstrous phantoms; all men do. And inside and outside the wind blows. But when the time comes, like now, then the storm around me does not matter. The winds within me do not matter. Nothing human or earthly can touch me. A peace gathers in my heart. What seems unpossessable, I can possess. What seems unfathomable, I can fathom. What is unutterable, I can utter. Because I can pray. I can communicate. How do people endure anything on earth if they cannot have God?'

The storms of life will come and go, vary in their intensity and hit us at our worst moments, but the peace of God remains the same – constant, enduring, comforting. When we choose His peace over worry, fear and anxiety, our hearts and minds abide secure therein.

Persecution

Remember the word that I said to you, 'A servant is not greater than his master.' If they persecuted Me, they will also persecute you.

John 15:20 NKJV

Blessed are those who have been persecuted for the sake of righteousness, for theirs is the kingdom of heaven.

Matthew 5:10 NASB

Everyone who wants to live a godly life in Christ Jesus will suffer persecution.

2 Timothy 3:12 NLT

We are hard pressed on every side, but not crushed; perplexed, but not in despair; persecuted, but not abandoned; struck down, but not destroyed.

2 Corinthians 4:8–9 NIV

Persecution

He's Holding You

Many years ago, a young woman who felt called into the ministry was accepted into a well-known theological college. There were only two other women enrolled there, and her very presence seemed to make her male classmates uncomfortable. She felt isolated. To make matters worse, many of her professors were doing their best to destroy her faith rather than build it up. Even her private devotions seemed dry and lonely.

At Christmas break she asked her father's advice. 'How can I be strong in my resolve and straight in my theology with all that I face there?'

Her father took a pencil from his pocket and laid it on the palm of his hand. 'Can that pencil stand upright by itself?' he asked her.

'No,' she replied. Then her father grasped the pencil in his hand and held it in an upright position. 'Ah,' she said, 'but you are holding it now.'

'Daughter,' he replied, 'your life is like this pencil. But Jesus Christ is the one who can hold you.' The young woman took her father's pencil and returned to college.

Whatever difficulties you may confront today, remember it is God who holds you in His hands. His strength holds you up and enables you to face anything that comes your way.

Persecution

God blesses you when you are mocked and persecuted and lied about because you are my followers.

Matthew 5:11 NLT

Who shall separate us from the love of Christ? Shall trouble or hardship or persecution or famine or nakedness or danger or sword? . . . No, in all these things we are more than conquerors through him who loved us.

Romans 8:35,37 NIV

I tell you to love your enemies and pray for anyone who mistreats you.

Matthew 5:44 CEV

Bless those who persecute you; bless and curse not.

Romans 12:14 NASB

A 'Why' to Live For

Victor Frankl was stripped of everything he owned when he was arrested by the Nazis in World War II. He arrived at Auschwitz with only his manuscrip – a book he had been researching and writing for years. Upon arrival, even that was taken from him. He later wrote, 'I had to undergo and overcome the loss of my spiritual child . . . It seemed as if nothing and no one would survive me. I found myself confronted with the question of whether under such circumstances my life was ultimately void of any meaning.'

Days later, the Nazis forced the prisoners to give up their clothes. In return Frankl was given the rags of an inmate who had been sent to the gas chamber. In the pocket of the garment he found a torn piece of paper – a page from a Hebrew prayer book. On it was the foremost Jewish prayer, 'Shema Yisrael' which begins, 'Hear, O Israel! The Lord our God is one God.'

Frankl says, 'How should I have interpreted such a "coincidence" other than as a challenge to live my thoughts instead of merely putting them on paper?' He later wrote in his classic masterpiece, *Man's Search for Meaning*, 'He who has a why to live for can bear almost any how.'

Perseverance

Consider it pure joy, my brothers, whenever you face trials of many kinds, because you know that the testing of your faith develops perseverance. Perseverance must finish its work so that you may be mature and complete, not lacking anything.

James 1:2–4 NIV

May the Master take you by the hand and lead you along the path of God's love and Christ's endurance.

2 Thessalonians 3:5 The Message

Love bears up under anything and everything that comes, is ever ready to believe the best of every person, its hopes are fadeless under all circumstances, and it endures everything [without weakening].

1 Corinthians 13:7 AMP

If anyone suffers as a Christian, let him not feel ashamed, but in that name let him glorify God.

1 Peter 4:16 NASB

Perseverance

Pressed, but not Crushed

Bathyspheres are amazing inventions. Operating like a miniature submarine, they have been used to explore the ocean in places so deep the water pressure would crush a conventional submarine as easily as if it were an aluminium can. Bathyspheres compensate for the intense water pressure with plates of steel several inches thick. The steel keeps the water out, but it also makes a bathysphere very heavy and difficult to manoeuvre. The space inside is cramped, allowing for only one or two people to survey the ocean floor by looking through a tiny plate-glass window.

What divers invariably find at every depth of the ocean are fish and other sea creatures! Some of these creatures are quite small and appear to have fairly normal skin. They look flexible and supple as they swim through the inky waters. How can they live at these depths without steel plating? They compensate for the outside pressure through equal and opposite pressure on the inside.

Spiritual fortitude works in the same way. The more negative the circumstances around us, the more we need to allow God's power to work within us to exert an equal and opposite pressure from the inside. With God in the inside, we can persevere in any situation and no pressure on earth can crush us!

Perseverance

We also glory in tribulations, knowing that
tribulation produces perseverance; and perseverance, character; and character, hope.

Romans 5:3–4 NKJV

You need to persevere so that when you have
done the will of God, you will receive what he
has promised.

Hebrews 10:36 NIV

The good soil represents honest, good-hearted
people who hear God's message, cling to it, and
steadily produce a huge harvest.

Luke 8:15 NLT

Pray at all times in the Spirit, with all prayer and
supplication. To that end keep alert with all perseverance, making supplication for all the saints.

Ephesians 6:18 RSV

Perseverance

We Can Get Bigger!

In the 1920s, an English adventurer named Mallory led an expedition to try to conquer Mt. Everest. His first expedition failed. So did the second. Mallory made a third attempt with a highly skilled and experienced team, but in spite of careful planning and extensive safety measures, an avalanche wiped out Mallory and most of his party. Upon their return to England, the few who had survived held a banquet to salute Mallory and those who had perished on the mountain. As the leader of the survivors stood to speak, he looked around the hall at the framed pictures of Mallory and the others who had died. Then he turned his back to the crowd and faced a large picture of Mount Everest, which stood looming behind the banquet table like a silent, unbeatable giant.

With tears streaming down his face, he spoke to the mountain on behalf of his dead friends: 'I speak to you, Mt. Everest, in the name of all brave men living, and those yet unborn. Mt. Everest, you defeated us once; you defeated us twice; you defeated us three times. But, Mt. Everest, we shall someday defeat you, because you can't get any bigger and we can.'

Keep your enthusiasm. Keep persevering. Run your race until you cross the finish line!

Protection

I can lie down and sleep soundly because you,
LORD, will keep me safe.

Psalm 4:8 CEV

If you make the Most High your dwelling –
even the LORD, who is my refuge – then no
harm will befall you, no disaster will come near
your tent. For he will command his angels
concerning you to guard you in all your ways.

Psalm 91:9–11 NIV

No weapon turned against you will succeed.
And everyone who tells lies in court will be
brought to justice. These benefits are enjoyed
by the servants of the LORD; their vindication
will come from me. I, the LORD, have spoken!

Isaiah 54:17 NLT

Don't be afraid. I am with you. Don't tremble
with fear. I am your God. I will make you
strong, as I protect you with my arm and give
you victories.

Isaiah 41:10 CEV

Protection

Love Protects

When Salvation Army officer Shaw looked at the three men standing before him, he was moved to compassion. A medical missionary, Shaw had just been sent to a leper colony in India. The men before him wore manacles and fetters, the metal cutting into their diseased flesh. The Captain turned to their guard and said, 'Please unfasten the chains.' The guard immediately replied, 'It isn't safe. These men are dangerous criminals as well as lepers!'

Captain Shaw replied, 'I'll be responsible. They're suffering enough.' He personally took the keys, tenderly removed the bindings and treated their bleeding, decaying ankles and wrists.

Two weeks later, Shaw had his first misgiving about what he had done when he had to make an emergency overnight trip. He dreaded leaving his family alone in the colony, but his wife insisted she was not afraid – God would protect her. Shaw left as planned. The following morning his wife was startled to find the three criminals lying on their doorstep. One of them said, 'We know the doctor go. We stay here all night so no harm come to you.'

Shaw's belief in the love of God gave him the courage to loose the lepers. Shaw's courage gave the lepers the love to protect his family.

Protection

The LORD shall preserve you from all evil; He shall preserve your soul. The LORD shall preserve your going out and your coming in from this time forth, and even forevermore.

Psalm 121:7–8 NKJV

When you pass through the waters, I will be with you; and when you pass through the rivers, they will not sweep over you. When you walk through the fire, you will not be burned; the flames will not set you ablaze.

Isaiah 43:2 NIV

God's angel sets up a circle of protection around us while we pray.

Psalm 34:7 The Message

The name of the LORD is a strong fortress; the godly run to him and are safe.

Proverbs 18:10 NLT

Protection

A Real Traffic-Stopper

While driving along the motorway, the adults in the front seat of a car were talking when suddenly they heard the horrifying sound of a car door opening, the whistle of wind and a sickening thud. They quickly turned and saw that the three-year-old child riding in the back seat had fallen out of the car and was tumbling along the road. The driver screeched to a stop, then raced back towards her child. To her surprise, she found that all the traffic had stopped just a few feet away from her child. Her daughter had not been hit.

A truck driver took the girl to a nearby hospital. The doctors there rushed her into the emergency room, and soon came back with the good news: other than a few scrapes and bruises, the girl was fine. No broken bones. No apparent internal damage.

As the mother rushed to her child, the little girl opened her eyes and said, 'Mummy, you know I wasn't afraid. While I was lying on the road waiting for you to get back to me, I looked up and right there I saw Jesus holding back the traffic with His arms out.'

God watches over us with loving care.

Reconciliation

Pursue peace with all people, and holiness, without which no one will see the Lord: looking carefully lest anyone fall short of the grace of God; lest any root of bitterness springing up cause trouble, and by this many become defiled.

Hebrews 12:14–15 NKJV

Blessed are the merciful: for they shall obtain mercy.

Matthew 5:7 KJV

Do not be overcome by evil, but overcome evil with good.

Romans 12:21 NIV

Be kind to each other, tenderhearted, forgiving one another, just as God through Christ has forgiven you.

Ephesians 4:32 NLT

Reconciliation

Warm Reconciliation

Years after her experience in a Nazi concentration camp, Corrie ten Boom found herself standing face to face with one of the most cruel and heartless German guards she had met while in the camps. This man had humiliated and degraded both her and her sister.

Now he stood before her with an outstretched hand, asking, 'Will you forgive me?' Corrie said, 'I stood there with coldness clutching at my heart, but I know that the will can function regardless of the temperature of the heart. I prayed, "Jesus, help me!" Woodenly, mechanically, I thrust my hand into the one stretched out to me and I experienced an incredible thing. The current started in my shoulder, raced down into my arm and sprang into our clutched hands. Then this warm reconciliation seemed to flood my whole being, bringing tears to my eyes. "I forgive you, brother," I cried with my whole heart. For a long moment we grasped each other's hands, the former guard, the former prisoner. I have never known the love of God so intensely as I did in that moment!'

When we choose to extend mercy to another, God's great mercy and love warms and softens our hearts once more. We are freed when we free another.

Reconciliation

The discretion of a man makes him slow to anger, And his glory is to overlook a transgression.

Proverbs 19:11 NKJV

Do not resist an evil person. If someone strikes you on the right cheek, turn to him the other also.

Matthew 5:39 NIV

Whenever you stand praying, forgive, if you have anything against any one; so that your Father also who is in heaven may forgive you your trespasses.

Mark 11:25 RSV

If your brother sins against you, rebuke him; and if he repents, forgive him.

Luke 17:3 NKJV

Reconciliation

Silence Beyond Words

Marie Louise de La Ramee says in *Ouida*, 'There are many moments in friendship, as in love, when silence is beyond words. The faults of our friend may be clear to us, but it is well to seem to shut our eyes to them.

'Friendship is usually treated by the majority of mankind as a tough and everlasting thing which will survive all manner of bad treatment. But this is an exceedingly great and foolish error; it may die in an hour of a single unwise word.'

If the words 'I love you' are the most important three words in a marriage, the words 'I'm sorry' are probably the *two* most important! The more a spouse is willing to admit fault, the greater the likelihood the other spouse will also grow to be vulnerable enough to admit error. That doesn't mean a person should apologize for an error that has not been made; to do so would be to become a doormat or to manifest a false humility. When one is standing in the right, although the other cannot see it, the better approach is silence. Not saying, 'I'm not speaking to you until you apologize,' but saying nothing more about the issue. Remember, silence is golden.

Rejection

Behold what manner of love the Father has bestowed on us, that we should be called children of God! Therefore the world does not know us, because it did not know Him.

1 John 3:1 NKJV

A man of many companions may come to ruin, but there is a friend who sticks closer than a brother.

Proverbs 18:24 NIV

Long ago, even before he made the world, God loved us and chose us in Christ to be holy and without fault in his eyes.

Ephesians 1:4 NLT

For the LORD will not forsake his people; he will not abandon his heritage; for justice will return to the righteous, and all the upright in heart will follow it.

Psalm 94:14–15 RSV

Rejection

Overcoming Rejection

John Hull, author of *Touching the Rock*, is blind.
In telling his life story, he recounts that his
mother spent two years attending Melbourne
High School, lodging there with Mildred
Treloar. While living with her, John's mother
began attending weekly Bible classes with her.
Over the months, her personal dedication to the
Lord was renewed and deepened as the pages of
the Bible came alive for her. It was this vibrant
faith that she passed to her son, John.

Where did Mildred Treloar acquire her
faith? From her father. Mr Treloar had desired
to become a minister as a young man, but was
rejected by his denomination. Rather than
become bitter, he poured his faith into Mildred.
While she lived with Mildred, John's mother
spent many hours reading the Bible to Mr
Treloar and vividly recalled for John his great
hope of heaven. Why was Mr Treloar considered to be unacceptable as a minister? He was
blind!

If Mr Treloar had given in to bitterness or
self-pity when his denomination rejected him,
he could not have passed such vibrant faith on
to his daughter. When we're rejected, we can
overcome it by turning to God, instead of away
from Him. He will never reject us!

Rejection

The poor and needy seek water, but there is none, their tongues fail for thirst. I, the LORD, will hear them; I, the God of Israel, will not forsake them.

Isaiah 41:17 NKJV

And Jesus said, 'Neither do I condemn you; go your way. From now on sin no more.'

John 8:11 NASB

He was despised and rejected – a man of sorrows, acquainted with bitterest grief. We turned our backs on him and looked the other way when he went by. He was despised, and we did not care.

Isaiah 53:3 NLT

Heart-shattered lives ready for love don't for a moment escape God's notice.

Psalm 51:17 The Message

Rejection

Pushing Past Rejection

Sparky didn't have much going for him. He failed every subject in the eighth grade, and in high school, he flunked Latin, algebra, English and physics. He made the golf team, but promptly lost the most important match of the season, and then lost the consolation match. He was awkward socially. While in high school, he never once asked a girl to go out on a date.

Only one thing was important to Sparky – drawing. He was proud of his artwork even though no one else appreciated it. He submitted cartoons to the editors of his high school year-book, but they were turned down. Even so, Sparky aspired to be an artist. After high school, he sent samples of his artwork to the Walt Disney Studios. Again, he was turned down.

Still, Sparky didn't give up! He decided to write his own autobiography in cartoons. The character he created became famous worldwide – the subject not only of cartoon strips but countless books, television shows and licensing opportunities. Sparky, you see, was Charles Schulz, creator of the *Peanuts* comic strip. Like his character, Charlie Brown, Schulz may not have been able to do many things. But, rather than letting rejection stop him, he made the most of what he could do!

Relationships

But if we walk in the light, as he is in the light, we have fellowship with one another, and the blood of Jesus, his Son, purifies us from all sin.

1 John 1:7 NIV

The Scripture was fulfilled which says, 'Abraham believed God, and it was accounted to him for righteousness.' And he was called the friend of God.

James 2:23 NKJV

Now I tell you to love each other, as I have loved you. The greatest way to show love for friends is to die for them. And you are my friends, if you obey me.

John 15:12–14 CEV

Friends love through all kinds of weather, and families stick together in all kinds of trouble.

Proverbs 17:17 The Message

Relationships

Wars and Rumours of Wars

A little girl once asked her father how wars got started.

'Well,' said her father, 'suppose America persisted in quarrelling with England, and . . .'

'But,' interrupted her mother, 'America must never quarrel with England.'

'I know,' said the father, 'but I am only using a hypothetical instance.'

'But you are misleading the child,' protested Mum.

'No, I am not,' replied the father indignantly, with an edge of anger in his tone.

'Never mind, Daddy,' the little girl interjected, 'I think I know how wars get started.'

Most major arguments don't begin major, but are rooted in small annoyances, breaches or trespasses. It's like the mighty oak that stood on the skyline of the Rocky Mountains. The tree had survived hail, heavy snows, bitter cold and ferocious storms for more than a century. It was finally felled not by a great lightning strike or an avalanche, but by an attack of tiny beetles.

A little hurt, neglect or insult can be the beginning of the end for virtually any relationship. Therefore, take care what you say, check your attitude and be quick to ask for forgiveness when you've been wrong. Maintain those important relationships in your life and don't let the 'tiny beetles' eat away at them.

Relationships

Do not forsake your friend and the friend of
your father.

Proverbs 27:10 NIV

Therefore if you bring your gift to the altar, and
there remember that your brother has something against you, leave your gift there before
the altar, and go your way. First be reconciled to
your brother, and then come and offer your
gift.

Matthew 5:23–24 NKJV

Stay on good terms with each other, held
together by love.

Hebrews 13:1 The Message

Do not be bound together with unbelievers; for
what partnership have righteousness and law-
lessness, or what fellowship has light with darkness?

2 Corinthians 6:14 NASB

Relationships

The Legend of David's Temple

Most authorities believe King David's temple was built on Mount Moriah, the mount where Abraham was told to sacrifice Isaac. But there's another Hebrew legend that presents a different story.

The legend says that two brothers lived on adjoining farms, which were divided from the peak to the base of the mountain. The younger brother lived alone, unmarried. The older brother had a large family.

One night during the grain harvest, the older brother awoke and thought, *My brother is all alone. To cheer his heart, I will take some of my sheaves and lay them on his side of the field.*

At the same hour, the younger brother awoke and thought, *My brother has a large family and greater needs than I do. As he sleeps, I'll put some of my sheaves on his side of the field.* Each brother went out carrying sheaves to the other's field and they met halfway. When they declared their intentions to one another, they dropped their sheaves and embraced. It is at that place, the legend claims, the temple was built.

Whether this story is true or not, it exemplifies the highest expression of love – giving. Giving is one of life's best relationship-builders.

Renewal

And do not be conformed to this world, but be transformed by the renewing of your mind, that you may prove what is that good and acceptable and perfect will of God.

Romans 12:2 NKJV

A new heart I will give you, and a new spirit I will put within you; and I will take out of your flesh the heart of stone and give you a heart of flesh. And I will put my spirit within you, and cause you to walk in my statutes and be careful to observe my ordinances.

Ezekiel 36:26–27 RSV

If we confess our sins, he is faithful and just to forgive us our sins, and to cleanse us from all unrighteousness.

1 John 1:9 KJV

God, make a fresh start in me, shape a Genesis week from the chaos of my life.

Psalm 51:10 The Message

Renewal

Renewed in God's Strength

On February 11, 1861, President-elect Lincoln left his home in Springfield to begin his journey to Washington, where he was to be inaugurated a month later. Lincoln had a premonition it would be the last time he would see Springfield. Standing on the rear platform of his railroad car, he bid the townspeople farewell. He closed his remarks with these words: 'Today I leave you. I go to assume a task more difficult than that which devolved upon General Washington. The great God which guided him must help me. Without that assistance I shall surely fail; with it, I cannot fail.'

The same is true for us, regardless of the tasks we face. Without God's assistance, we cannot succeed. We may get the dishes washed, the laundry folded and the beds made. We may get our work done without accident or incident. We may find what we need at the market and manage to keep a schedule. But without God's help, our lives would still be a confused mess.

Does God care about what happens in our day? Absolutely! When we become overwhelmed, seeing the smallest tasks as giant mountains, He helps us to 'gather ourselves'. Step by step He shows us the way and renews our strength that we may go on.

Renewal

Therefore if any man be in Christ, he is a new creature: old things are passed away; behold, all things are become new.

2 Corinthians 5:17 KJV

Be made new in the attitude of your minds; and ... put on the new self, created to be like God in true righteousness and holiness.

Ephesians 4:23–24 NIV

My friends, I don't feel that I have already arrived. But I forget what is behind, and I struggle for what is ahead. I run toward the goal, so that I can win the prize of being called to heaven.

Philippians 3:13–14 CEV

Do not lie to one another, since you have put off the old man with his deeds, and have put on the new man who is renewed in knowledge according to the image of Him who created him.

Colossians 3:9–10 NKJV

Renewal

Rescue Me

Can the Lord speak through a pop song?
Fontella Bass thinks so. During 1990, she was at
the lowest point in her life. It had been twenty-
five years since her rhythm-and-blues single had
hit number one on the charts. She had no career
to speak of and she was broke, tired and cold.
The only heat in her tiny house came from a gas
stove in the kitchen. She had also strayed far
from the church where she had started singing
gospel songs as a child.

Fontella says, 'I said a long prayer. I said, "I
need to see a sign to continue on." ' No sooner
had she prayed than she heard her hit song,
Rescue Me, on a television commercial! To her, it
was as if 'the Lord had stepped right into my
world!'

Fontella was unaware that American
Express had been using her song as part of a
commercial. Officials had been unable to locate
her to pay her royalties. Not only did she receive
back-royalties but new opportunities for her to
sing began to open.

When we cry out to God because we've realized the futility of our own efforts, He renews
our hope and brings us blessings far greater
than we could have imagined.

Restoration

Restore to me the joy of thy salvation, and uphold me with a willing spirit ... The sacrifice acceptable to God is a broken spirit; a broken and contrite heart, O God, thou wilt not despise.

Psalm 51:12,17 RSV

Our God, make us strong again! Smile on us and save us.

Psalm 80:3 CEV

Turn us back to You, O LORD, and we will be restored; Renew our days as of old.

Lamentations 5:21 NKJV

And the God of all grace, who called you to his eternal glory in Christ, after you have suffered a little while, will himself restore you and make you strong, firm and steadfast.

1 Peter 5:10 NIV

Restoration

This Old Heart

At a crucial transition time in her life, a Christian woman cried out to the Lord, despairing over the lack of spiritual power she was experiencing in her life. Suddenly she sensed Jesus standing beside her, asking, 'May I have the keys to your life?'

The experience was so real, the woman reached into her pocket and took out a ring of keys. 'Are all the keys here?' the Lord asked.

'Yes, except the key to one small room in my life.'

'If you cannot trust Me in all rooms of your life, I cannot accept any of the keys.'

The woman was so overwhelmed at the thought of the Lord moving out of her life altogether, she cried, 'Lord! Take the keys to all the rooms of my life!'

Many of us have rooms we hope no one will ever see. We intend to clean them out someday, but someday never seems to come. When we invite Jesus into these rooms, He will clean them and restore them. With Him, we have the courage to throw away all the junk, and He will fill the rooms with His love and peace and joy. His grace beautifies the rooms and He makes Himself at home there.

Restoration

He restores my soul.

Psalm 23:3 NKJV

Change your life. Turn to God and be baptized, each of you, in the name of Jesus Christ, so your sins are forgiven. Receive the gift of the Holy Spirit.

Acts 2:38 The Message

Cast away from you all the transgressions that you have committed against me, and get yourselves a new heart and a new spirit!

Ezekiel 18:31 NRSV

So turn to God! Give up your sins, and you will be forgiven. Then that time will come when the Lord will give you fresh strength.

Acts 3:19–20 CEV

Restoration

The Lord is My Pacesetter

Not one of us automatically has time to pray.
We have to make time for prayer – carving a
time out of our day and setting it aside as a
sacred appointment that cannot be changed and
must not be delayed, for that's where we find
restoration and strength. As you set aside your
prayer time for today, consider this Japanese
version of the 23rd Psalm:

The Lord is my pacesetter . . . I shall not rush
He makes me stop for quiet intervals
He provides me with images of stillness,
   which restore my serenity
He leads me in the way of efficiency through
   calmness of mind and His guidance is peace
Even though I have a great many things to
   accomplish each day, I will not fret,
   for His presence is here
His timelessness, His all-importance will keep
   me in balance
He prepares refreshment and renewal in the
   midst of my activity by anointing my mind
   with the oils of tranquillity
My cup of joyous energy overflows
Truly harmony and effectiveness shall be the
   fruits of my hours
For I shall walk in the Pace of my Lord and
   dwell in His house for ever.

By walking in the Lord's pace, we are
restored moment by moment.

Self-Worth

You formed my inward parts; You covered me in my mother's womb. I will praise You, for I am fearfully and wonderfully made; Marvelous are Your works, And that my soul knows very well.

Psalm 139:13–14 NKJV

Put on the new self, which in the likeness of God has been created in righteousness and holiness of the truth.

Ephesians 4:24 NASB

'For I know the plans I have for you,' declares the LORD, 'plans to prosper you and not to harm you, plans to give you hope and a future.'

Jeremiah 29:11 NIV

And since we are his children, we will share his treasures – for everything God gives to his Son, Christ, is ours, too.

Romans 8:17 NLT

Self-Worth

Seeds of Self-Respect

A businessman hurriedly plonked a pound into the cup of a man who was selling flowers on a street corner and rushed away. Halfway down the street, he suddenly whirled about and made his way back to the beggar. 'I'm sorry,' he said, picking out a flower from the bunch that the beggar had in a bucket beside him. 'In my haste I failed to make my purchase. After all, you are a businessman just like me. Your merchandise is fairly priced and of good quality. I trust you won't be upset with my failure to take more care in my purchase.' And with that, the businessman smiled and walked away, flower in hand.

At lunch a few weeks later, the businessman was approached by a neatly dressed, well-groomed man who introduced himself and then said, 'I'm sure you don't remember me, and I don't even know your name, but your face is one I will never forget. You are the man who inspired me to make something of myself. I was a vagrant selling wilted flowers until you gave me back my self-respect. Now I believe I am a businessman.'

Self-respect is vital to every person. Purpose in your heart to build up the respect and self-esteem of others. In so doing, you'll be building more respect for yourself!

Self-Worth

How great is the love the Father has lavished on us, that we should be called children of God!
1 John 3:1 NIV

I have loved you with an everlasting love; therefore with loving-kindness have I drawn you.
Jeremiah 31:3 AMP

But God has given us his Spirit. That's why we don't think the same way that the people of this world think. That's also why we can recognize the blessings that God has given us.
1 Corinthians 2:12 CEV

He chose us in Him before the foundation of the world, that we should be holy and without blame before Him in love, having predestined us to adoption as sons by Jesus Christ to Himself, according to the good pleasure of His will, to the praise of the glory of His grace, by which He made us accepted in the Beloved.
Ephesians 1:4–6 NKJV

Self-Worth

Building Your Child's Self-Worth

A banker was appalled when his awkward teenage son began wearing ragged clothing and an earring in his ear. His first impulse was to demand that his son 'shape up and clean up'. But before he said anything, he thought, *My son must feel that he isn't a part of the school crowd. He's dressing this way to feel accepted. Rather than work on his dress, I need to work on his self-esteem.*

So a few weeks later, the father invited his son to go with him to his annual banker's club banquet. The two had a great time. Even though the son sported an orange streak in his hair, he wore a suit to the event and behaved superbly, recalling the names of his father's friends and confidently conversing with them. He had responded to the unspoken message of his father's invitation: 'Son, I'm proud of you.'

Criticism wounds and tears down. Praise heals and builds up. Your child will encounter plenty of criticism in his or her life, without any of it coming from you. An important part of raising a child is to literally raise their self-worth, their sights, and their faith. That kind of raising is the product of praising.

Shame

Fear not; you will no longer live in shame.

Isaiah 54:4 NLT

Indeed, let no one who waits on You be ashamed; let those be ashamed who deal treacherously without cause.

Psalm 25:3 NKJV

May those who hope in you not be disgraced because of me, O Lord, the LORD Almighty; may those who seek you not be put to shame.

Psalm 69:6 NIV

Behold I am laying in Zion a Stone that will make men stumble, a Rock that will make them fall; but he who believes in Him [who adheres to, trusts in and relies on Him] shall not be put to shame nor be disappointed in his expectations.

Romans 9:33 AMP

Shame

Forgiveness Erases Shame

As college roommates, Meg and Ann also became best friends. Then one day, Meg told Ann that John had asked her for a date. Ann was disappointed; she'd had a crush on John for two years. Still, she managed to say, 'Have a good time,' and later, to put on a happy face at John and Meg's wedding.

Through the years, Meg kept the relationship with Ann close. Ann enjoyed teasing and laughing with John. When Meg asked Ann to join them at a beachside bungalow for a week, Ann jumped at the chance. One afternoon when Meg went out to visit a friend, Ann and John betrayed Meg's trust. Afterwards, Ann felt sick inside. Deep shame welled up within her.

A few minutes of flirtation and passion resulted in more than a decade of misery for Ann. She might never have known happiness again if Meg hadn't confronted her about her refusal to accept a marriage proposal. Ann sobbed, 'I'm horrible. You don't know how I've wronged you.' Meg said, 'I do know, Ann,' and one look into her eyes confirmed that Meg had known, had loved and had forgiven. With that forgiveness, years of shameful pain melted away.

Shame

There is therefore now no condemnation for those who are in Christ Jesus.

Romans 8:1 NASB

Don't be ashamed to suffer for being a Christian. Praise God that you belong to him.

1 Peter 4:16 CEV

For I am not ashamed of the gospel of Christ, for it is the power of God to salvation for everyone who believes.

Romans 1:16 NKJV

Word hard so God can approve you. Be a good worker, one who does not need to be ashamed and who correctly explains the word of truth.

2 Timothy 2:15 NLT

Shame

Down in the Mire

D. L. Moody told the story of a Chinese convert who gave this testimony: 'I was down in a deep pit, half sunk in the mire, crying for someone to help me out. As I looked up I saw a venerable, gray-haired man looking down at me. I said, "Can you help me out?" "My son," he replied, "I am Confucius. If you had read my books and followed what I taught, you would never have fallen into this dreadful pit."

'I was beginning to sink into despair when I saw another figure above me. "My child," He said, "what is the matter?" But before I could reply, He was down in the mire by my side. He folded His arms about me and lifted me up and then fed and rested me. When I was well He did not say, "Shame on you for falling into that pit." Instead He said, "We will walk on together now." And we have been walking together until this day.'

No one can pray for you with greater insight or compassion than Jesus – and the Bible says He is continually making intercession to the Father on your behalf. He doesn't condemn you when you've failed, He climbs right in to your failure with you and gently pulls you out.

Stewardship

He who is faithful in what is least is faithful also in much; and he who is unjust in what is least is unjust also in much.

Luke 16:10 NKJV

Now it is required that those who have been given a trust must prove faithful.

1 Corinthians 4:2 NIV

God has given gifts to each of you from his great variety of spiritual gifts. Manage them well so that God's generosity can flow through you.

1 Peter 4:10 NLT

The good person is generous and lends lavishly; no shuffling or stumbling around for this one, but a sterling and solid and lasting reputation.

Psalm 112:5–6 The Message

Stewardship

Reaping a Harvest

The late Spencer Penrose, whose brother was a major political leader in Philadelphia in the late nineteenth century, was considered the 'black sheep' of the family. He chose to live in the West, instead of the East. In 1891, fresh out of Harvard, he made his way to Colorado Springs. Not long after his move, he wired his brother for $1500 so that he might go into a mining venture. His brother telegraphed him $150 instead – enough for the train fare home – and warned him against the deal.

Years later, Spencer returned to Philadelphia and handed his brother $75,000 in gold coins – payment, he said, for his 'investment' in his mining operation. His brother was stunned. He had qualms about accepting the money, however, and reminded his brother that he had advised against the venture and had only given him $150. 'That,' replied Spencer, 'is why I'm only giving you $75,000. If you had sent me the full $1500 I requested, I would be giving you three-quarters of a million dollars.'

Nothing invested, nothing gained. Every harvest requires an initial seed. Be generous in your seed sowing. Plant in good ground, and you can anticipate a good return. That's the secret of good stewardship.

Stewardship

A poor widow came, and put in two copper coins, which make a penny. And he called his disciples to him, and said to them, 'Truly, I say to you, this poor widow has put in more than all those who are contributing to the treasury. For they all contributed out of their abundance; but she out of her poverty has put in everything she had, her whole living.'

Mark 12:42–44 RSV

When you give to the needy, do not let your left hand know what your right hand is doing, so that your giving may be in secret.

Matthew 6:3–4 NIV

Command those who are rich in this present age not to be haughty, nor to trust in uncertain riches but in the living God, who gives us richly all things to enjoy.

1 Timothy 6:17 NKJV

Moreover, it is required of stewards that one be found trustworthy.

1 Corinthians 4:2 NASB

Stewardship

Stewardship vs. Misership

Someone once noted these eight reasons for a woman to buy an item: because her husband said she couldn't have it; it made her look thin; it came from Paris; the neighbours couldn't afford it; no one else had it; everyone had it; it was different; and just because.

Consider the example, however, of Bill Hughes, a shipyard worker. London tax officials thought they could prove Hughes was involved in illegal activity when they found he had a savings account of £9,000, yet earned only £30 a week. Instead, Hughes told them his 'secrets': He never ate sweets, smoked, drank or went out with women. He shaved with his brother's razor blades, charged his grandmother 12 per cent interest on money she borrowed from him, worked a night shift, and wore his father's shoes to save on shoe leather. He also went thirteen years without buying a new suit, never bought a single flower, only saw one movie in his entire life, ate everything served to him at mealtimes even if he didn't want it, and patched everything he owned until the patches wouldn't hold (including his underwear).

There is a balance to be found between spending too much and spending too little! Don't be a miser, be wiser. Enjoy life!

Strength

The LORD is my strength and song, and he is become my salvation: he is my God, and I will prepare him an habitation; my father's God, and I will exalt him.

Exodus 15:2 KJV

The LORD gives his people strength. The LORD blesses them with peace.

Psalm 29:11 NLT

My grace is sufficient for you, for My strength is made perfect in weakness.

2 Corinthians 12:9 NKJV

God is strong, and he wants you strong. So take everything the Master has set out for you, well-made weapons of the best materials. And put them to use so you will be able to stand up to everything the Devil throws your way.

Ephesians 6:10–11 The Message

Strength

Amazing Strength

A young woman was running a race, and she found herself falling further and further behind her competitors. Her friends cheered her on from the sidelines, but to no avail. Then suddenly, her lips began to move, her legs picked up speed, and to the amazement of the entire crowd watching the race, she passed her competitors one by one – and won the race!

After she had received her award and received the congratulations of her coach and teammates, she turned to her friends. One of them asked, 'We could see your lips moving but we couldn't make out what you were saying. What were you mumbling out there?'

The young woman replied, 'Oh, I was talking to God. I told Him, "Lord, You pick 'em up and I'll put 'em down. . . . You pick 'em up and I'll put 'em down."'

When we live our lives the way we know God's Word commands us, and we are believing to the best of our ability that the Lord will help us, we are then in a position to know with certainty what the Apostle Paul knew: 'I can do all things through Christ which strengtheneth me' (Philippians 4:13).

Strength

The LORD is my strength and my song; he has become my salvation.

Psalm 118:14 NIV

Behold, God is my salvation; I will trust, and will not be afraid; for the LORD God is my strength and my song, and he has become my salvation.

Isaiah 12:2 RSV

Sing aloud to God our strength; Make a joyful shout to the God of Jacob.

Psalm 81:1 NKJV

My body and mind may fail, but you are my strength and my choice forever.

Psalm 73:26 CEV

Strength

Our Refuge and Strength

Norma Zimmer had a difficult childhood as a result of her parents' drinking. Singing was her way to escape. As a high school senior, Norma was invited to be a featured soloist at the University Christian Church in Seattle. When her parents heard she was going to sing, they both insisted on attending the service. She says about that morning, 'I stole glances at the congregation, trying to find my parents ... then in horror I saw them – weaving down the aisle. They were late. The congregation stared. I don't know how I ever got through that morning.'

After she sang and took her seat, her heart pounding, the pastor preached: 'God is our refuge and strength, a tested help in time of trouble.' She says, 'My own trouble seemed to bear down on me with tremendous weight ... I realized how desperate life in our family was without God ... Jesus came into my life not only as Savior but for daily strength and direction.'

The salvation God offers us is not only for our future benefit, but for our day-to-day needs in the present. He is an ever-present help in times of trouble. Daily rely on Him for peace and direction – *He* is your refuge and your strength.

Stress

You will keep in perfect peace him whose mind is steadfast, because he trusts in you. Trust in the LORD for ever, for the LORD, the LORD, is the Rock eternal.

Isaiah 26:3–4 NIV

Come to Me, all you who labor and are heavy laden, and I will give you rest.

Matthew 11:28 NKJV

May the Lord of peace himself always give you his peace no matter what happens. The Lord be with you all.

2 Thessalonians 3:16 NLT

And let the peace of Christ rule in your hearts, to which indeed you were called in the one body. And be thankful.

Colossians 3:15 NRSV

Stress

Foolproof Therapy

In *Growing Strong in the Seasons of Life,* Charles
Swindoll writes: 'Tonight was fun 'n' games
night around the supper table in our house. It
was wild. First of all, one of the kids snickered
during the prayer (which isn't that unusual)
and that tipped the first domino. Then a
humorous incident from school was shared and
the event (as well as how it was told) triggered
havoc around the table. That was the beginning
of twenty to thirty minutes of the loudest, silli-
est, most enjoyable laughter you can imagine. At
one point I watched my oldest literally fall off
his chair in hysterics, my youngest doubled over
in his chair as his face wound up in his plate
with corn chips stuck to his cheeks ... and my
two girls leaning back, lost and preoccupied in
the most beautiful and beneficial therapy God
ever granted humanity: laughter.

'What is so amazing is that everything
seemed far less serious and heavy. Irritability
and impatience were ignored like unwanted
guests. For example, during the meal little
Chuck spilled his drink twice ... and even that
brought the house down.'

What a treasure laughter is. It completely
dissipates anxiety, erases stress, and relieves
fears. It's the best antidote for stress there is!

Stress

I will listen to what God the LORD will say; he promises peace to his people, his saints.

Psalm 85:8 NIV

Great peace have they which love thy law: and nothing shall offend them.

Psalm 119:165 KJV

Think of the bright future waiting for all the families of honest and innocent and peace-loving people.

Psalm 37:37 CEV

And God's peace [shall be yours, that tranquil state of a soul assured of its salvation through Christ, and so fearing nothing from God and content with its earthly lot of whatever sort that is, that peace] which transcends all understanding, shall garrison and mount guard over your hearts and minds in Christ Jesus.

Philippians 4:7 AMP

Stress

Pray Your Stress Away

Claire Townsend found the weekly production meetings at the major motion picture studio where she worked to be extremely stressful. All morning, various department heads would jockey for position. The studio had just been bought out, jobs were uncertain and team spirit had vanished. To counteract the stress, Claire began to spend more time on her spiritual life. She began to pray again, discovering the power of God's love in her life. Even so, she dreaded this weekly battle.

Then one day during a particularly tense meeting, the thought came to her, *Pray. Pray now.* She began to imagine God's love pulsating within her, and then shooting out from her heart like a beam. She aimed her 'love laser' towards the person sitting across from her. The co-worker eyed her curiously and Claire smiled back. One by one, she beamed God's love to each person around the table as she silently prayed. Within minutes, the tone of the meeting changed from confrontation to compromise. As the group relaxed, they became more creative, and Claire began to regard the meetings as an opportunity to impart God's love.

In the midst of a stressful situation, turn to God. When we shift our focus to His love for us and others, our stress is replaced with peace.

Success

True humility and fear of the LORD lead to riches, honor, and long life.

Proverbs 22:4 NLT

Suppose you are very rich and able to enjoy everything you own. Then go ahead and enjoy working hard – this is God's gift to you.

Ecclesiastes 5:19 CEV

You will decide on a matter, and it will be established for you, and light will shine on your ways.

Job 22:28 RSV

Wealth and Glory accompany me – also substantial Honor and a Good Name.

Proverbs 8:18 The Message

Success

God's Work – God's Pay

As a young man, J.C. Penney ran a butcher shop. He was told that if he gave a fifth of Scotch to the head chef in a popular hotel, the business of that hotel would be his. Penney did this for some time. Then he felt convicted that what he was doing was wrong. He discontinued the gifts of liquor and sure enough, lost the hotel's business, causing him to go broke. God, however, had better things planned for him. In time, he began a merchandise business that grew into a nationwide enterprise.

Unsuccessful years alone don't create success. Remaining true to principles and doing the right thing – even when you seem to be failing – produce success in time. A poem by an unknown writer says it well:

Who does God's work will get God's pay,
However long may seem the day,
However weary be the way;
Though powers and princes thunder 'Nay',
Who does God's work will get God's pay.
He does not pay as others pay,
In gold or land or raiment gay;
In goods that vanish and decay;
But God in wisdom knows a way,
And that is sure, let come what may,
Who does God's work will get God's pay.

Success

People should eat and drink and enjoy the fruits of their labor, for these are gifts from God.

Ecclesiastes 3:13 NLT

Wealth and riches are in his house, and his righteousness endures for ever.

Psalm 112:3 NIV

The LORD your God will make you abound in all the work of your hand, in the fruit of your body, in the increase of your livestock, and in the produce of your land for good.

Deuteronomy 30:9 NKJV

They are like trees growing beside a stream, trees that produce fruit in season and always have leaves. Those people succeed in everything they do.

Psalm 1:3 CEV

Success

True Success

Jenny Lind was known as 'The Swedish Nightingale' during her very successful career as an operatic singer. She became one of the wealthiest artists of her time, yet she left the stage at her peak and never returned.

Countless people speculated as to the reason for her leaving, and most people wondered how she could give up so much applause, fame and money. However, she was content to live in privacy in a home by the sea.

One day a friend found her on the beach, her Bible on her knees, looking out into the glorious glow of a sunset. As they talked, the friend asked, 'Madame, how is it that you ever came to abandon the stage at the height of your success?'

She answered quietly, 'When every day it made me think less of this (laying a finger on her Bible) and nothing at all of that (pointing to the sunset), what else could I do?'

The world may never understand your decision to follow God's way. But then, perhaps God cannot understand a decision to pursue what the world offers when He has such great rewards in store for those who follow Him. True success is found in knowing and loving God.

Suffering

He is despised and rejected by men, a Man of sorrows and acquainted with grief. And we hid, as it were, our faces from Him; He was despised, and we did not esteem Him.

Isaiah 53:3 NKJV

He then began to teach them that the Son of Man must suffer many things and be rejected by the elders, chief priests and teachers of the law, and that he must be killed and after three days rise again.

Mark 8:31 NIV

For as the sufferings of Christ abound in us, so our consolation also abounds through Christ.

2 Corinthians 1:5 NKJV

I am sure that what we are suffering now cannot compare with the glory that will be shown to us.

Romans 8:18 CEV

Suffering

Peace in the Midst of Suffering

A minister once went to the hospital to visit a friend named Ruth. She and her husband had served as missionaries for more than twenty years. It seemed incongruous that this woman should now be suffering the final stages of inoperable lung cancer. She had never smoked. Rounds of agonizing chemotherapy had taken their toll and now even that treatment had been abandoned. Ruth was left to wait for inevitable death. The minister quickly prayed about what he might say to her.

Other than her loss of hair, Ruth showed no signs of advanced cancer. She radiated peace as she began to tell the minister how thankful she was that God had allowed her to walk down this path of suffering. 'I've always been a Martha,' she said, 'too busy to sit at the feet of Jesus, but this cancer slowed me down so that I can get to know Him in ways I never did before.' The minister left her room encouraged, not downcast. He had been asking God why Ruth had to suffer. Meanwhile, Ruth was rejoicing in the midst of her experience!

God never causes our suffering, but when we look to Him, He can use it for our good.

Suffering

I delight in weaknesses, in insults, in hardships, in persecutions, in difficulties. For when I am weak, then I am strong.

2 Corinthians 12:10 NIV

Disciples so often get into trouble; still, God is there every time.

Psalm 34:19 The Message

Blessed is the man who endures temptation; for when he has been approved, he will receive the crown of life which the Lord has promised to those who love Him.

James 1:12 NKJV

Now that Jesus has suffered and was tempted, he can help anyone else who is tempted.

Hebrews 2:18 CEV

Suffering

Shine

One day while backpacking, Heidi doubled over with stomach pain. After being rushed to the hospital and undergoing surgery, she seemed to recover quickly. Then tests revealed an adrenal tumour. Heidi underwent more surgery, followed by extensive radiation. She asked her father, 'Why me, Dad?' Her father answered, 'Honey, I don't know. But the book of Matthew says, "Ye are the light of the world ... Let your light so shine before men, that they may see your good works, and glorify your Father which is in heaven." I know you have accepted Jesus as your personal Saviour and have become one of His lights. Just keep shining.'

Two years later, Paul watched his 'light' receive her high-school diploma, and then the cancer struck again, this time in her lungs. As Paul embraced his daughter, he could only say, 'Honey, all we can do is call on the Lord for His strength.' Another surgery followed, and the following Christmas Paul was again filled with joy when Heidi married. The following April, she died as a result of brain cancer.

Jesus suffered and died, so that He could be with us in all our suffering. He has experienced our sufferings and He enables us to shine on in the midst of them.

Temptation

Put on the whole armor of God, that you may be able to stand against the wiles of the devil.

Ephesians 6:11 NKJV

Be self-controlled and alert. Your enemy the devil prowls around like a roaring lion looking for someone to devour.

1 Peter 5:8 NIV

The Lord knows how to rescue the godly from temptation, and to keep the unrighteous under punishment for the day of judgment.

2 Peter 2:9 NASB

Stay awake and pray that you won't be tested. You want to do what is right, but you are weak.

Mark 14:38 CEV

Temptation

Escaping the Sirens

As the ancient myth goes, when Ulysses sailed out to meet the Sirens, he stopped his ears with wax and had himself bound to the mast of his ship. He was apparently unaware that every traveller before him had done the same thing and that wax and chains were no match for the Sirens. Their alluring song could pierce through anything, causing sailors to break all manner of bonds.

However, the Sirens had an even more fatal weapon than their song. Silence. As Ulysses approached, the Sirens chose to employ that weapon. Rather than be seduced into straining to hear their song though, Ulysses concluded that he must be the only person who could not hear their song and that he must be immune to their powers. Strengthened in that confidence, he set his gaze on the distant horizon and escaped the Sirens as no man before him.

Temptation always begins in what we see and what we hear. Choose carefully what your eyes see and what your ears hear. When you choose to keep your thoughts focused on God and His Word, setting your gaze on Him, He will show you what is good and help you resist temptation.

Temptation

No temptation has overtaken you that is not common to man. God is faithful, and he will not let you be tempted beyond your strength, but with the temptation will also provide the way of escape, that you may be able to endure it.

1 Corinthians 10:13 RSV

Since he himself has gone through suffering and temptation, he is able to help us when we are being tempted.

Hebrews 2:18 NLT

You are of God, little children, and have overcome them, because He who is in you is greater than he who is in the world.

1 John 4:4 NKJV

You obeyed my message and endured. So I will protect you from the time of testing that everyone in all the world must go through.

Revelation 3:10 CEV

Temptation

A Way of Escape

As a teenager, Megan arrived home from school just in time to watch an hour of soap operas before doing her homework. She enjoyed the escape into the TV world and wasn't really aware that the programmes were creating in her an inordinate amount of sexual curiosity. Over months and even years of watching her 'soaps', Megan's perspective on life shifted. She began to think, *Relationships don't need to be pure – in fact, the impure ones seem more exciting. Fidelity doesn't matter, as long as a person is 'happy'.*

As a college student, Megan found it easy to participate in 'one-night stands'. Then, after a short marriage ended in catastrophe as a result of her infidelity, she sought help from a counsellor. At the outset, it was difficult for the counsellor to understand why Megan had engaged in extramarital affairs. As far as her public behaviour was concerned, she had been a model teenager at home, at church and at school. Finally, the counsellor discovered the source of the temptation that drove Megan to participate in her hidden life.

We can avert temptation by avoiding those things that cause it. But we are human, and no matter how careful we are, we will be tempted. Yet God always provides a way of escape!

Thankfulness

Plant your roots in Christ and let him be the foundation for your life. Be strong in your faith, just as you were taught. And be grateful.

Colossians 2:7 CEV

Whatever you do or say, let it be as a representative of the Lord Jesus, all the while giving thanks through him to God the Father.

Colossians 3:17 NLT

Thanks be to God, who gives us the victory through our Lord Jesus Christ.

1 Corinthians 15:57 NASB

Thanks be to God, who always leads us in triumphal procession in Christ and through us spreads everywhere the fragrance of the knowledge of him.

2 Corinthians 2:14 NIV

Thankfulness

Thou Shalt Not Whine

Rather than whining because we don't have certain things in our lives or because we think something is wrong, we should take positive action.

Here are four steps for turning whining into thanksgiving:

1. *Give something away*. When you give, you create both a physical and a mental space for something new and better to come into your life. Although you may think you are 'lacking' something in life, when you give you demonstrate the abundance in your life.

2. *Narrow your goals*. Don't expect everything good to come into your life all at once. When you focus your expectations toward specific, attainable goals, you are more apt to direct your time and energy toward reaching them.

3. *Change your vocabulary from 'I need' to 'I want'*. Most of the things we think we need are actually things we want. When you receive them, you will be thankful for even small luxuries, rather than seeing them as necessities.

4. *Choose to be thankful for what you already have*. Thanksgiving is a choice. Every one of us has more things to be thankful for than we could even begin to recount in a single day.

Put these principles into practice – you will find yourself whining less and thanking God more.

Thankfulness

In everything give thanks; for this is the will of God in Christ Jesus for you.

1 Thessalonians 5:18 NKJV

Give thanks to the LORD, for he is good; his love endures for ever.

Psalm 107:1 NIV

You have turned my mourning into joyful dancing. You have taken away my clothes of mourning and clothed me with joy, that I might sing praises to you and not be silent. O LORD my God, I will give you thanks forever!

Psalm 30:11–12 NLT

O come, let us sing for joy to the LORD; Let us shout joyfully to the rock of our salvation. Let us come before His presence with thanksgiving.

Psalm 95:1–2 NASB

Thankfulness

It's All About Relationship

Imagine for a moment that someone you love comes to you and asks to borrow a small sum of money. You no doubt would lend it gladly, in part because of the close relationship you share.

Now imagine that this same person continues to come to you, asking for loans, food, clothing, the use of your car, a place to stay and to borrow tools and appliances. While you do love this person, you would probably begin to feel that something was wrong. It's not the asking, but the attitude.

What causes the dilemma in this type of situation? The person who is coming with requests no longer sees his friend as someone with thoughts and feelings, but as a source of goods and services. So often we come to God in prayer with our request list in hand – 'God, please do this . . .' or 'God, I want . . .' We are wise to reconsider our relationship with God in prayer. *Who is this One to Whom we pray? How good has He been to us? Doesn't He deserve our praise and thanksgiving?*

We are missing out on the incredible benefits of an intimate relationship with God when we always come to Him with an empty hand instead of a heart full of praise and thanksgiving.

Wisdom

I will praise the LORD, who counsels me; even at night my heart instructs me.

Psalm 16:7 NIV

The LORD grants wisdom! From his mouth come knowledge and understanding.

Proverbs 2:6 NLT

The foolishness of God is wiser than men, and the weakness of God is stronger than men.

1 Corinthians 1:25 RSV

God has chosen the foolish things of the world to shame the wise, and God has chosen the weak things of the world to shame the things which are strong.

1 Corinthians 1:27 NASB

Wisdom

Life Buoys

Sara Orne Jewett has written a beautiful novel about Maine, *The Country of the Pointed Firs*. In it, she describes the path that leads a woman writer from her home to that of a retired sea captain named Elijah Tilley. On the way, there are a number of wooden stakes in the ground that appear to be randomly scattered on his property. Each is painted white and trimmed in yellow, just like the captain's house.

Once she arrives at the captain's abode, the writer asks Captain Tilley what the stakes mean. He tells her that when he first made the transition from sailing the seas to ploughing the land, he discovered his plough would catch on many of the large rocks just beneath the surface of the ground. Recalling how buoys in the sea always marked trouble spots for him, he set out the stakes as 'land buoys' to mark the rocks. Then he could avoid ploughing over them in the future.

God's promises and commandments are like buoys for us, revealing the trouble spots and rocky points of life. When we follow the wisdom found in God's Word and thereby steer clear of what is harmful to us, life is not only more enjoyable, but more productive.

Wisdom

If you need wisdom – if you want to know what God wants you to do – ask him, and he will gladly tell you. He will not resent your asking.

James 1:5 NLT

The depth of the riches of the wisdom and knowledge of God! How unsearchable his judgments, and his paths beyond tracing out!

Romans 11:33 NIV

'Our God, your name will be praised forever and forever. You are all-powerful, and you know everything. You control human events – you give rulers their power and take it away, and you are the source of wisdom and knowledge.'

Daniel 2:20–21 CEV

The LORD by wisdom founded the earth; by understanding He established the heavens.

Proverbs 3:19 NKJV

Wisdom

Turn to God

When Dwight D. Eisenhower was Supreme Commander of the Allied invasion of Europe during World War II, he was faced with the responsibility of making one of the most far-reaching decisions ever posed to a single man: the decision to change the date of D-Day at the last moment. The consequences of a wrong decision were so overwhelming, in his opinion, that he felt crushed by the weight of the decision before him. Still, he was the Supreme Commander and the only man who could make the decision that would impact millions of lives. He later wrote:

'I knew I did not have the required wisdom. But I turned to God. I asked God to give me the wisdom. I yielded myself to Him. I surrendered myself. And He gave me clear guidance. He gave me insight to see what was right, and He endowed me with courage to make my decision. And finally He gave me peace of mind in the knowledge that, having been guided by God to the decision, I could leave the results to Him.'

Few decisions you face in life will ever approach that magnitude, but whatever size problem we face, God generously offers His wisdom. All we must do is ask.

Additional titles in this series are:

God's Little Lessons on Life
(0 86347 341 5)
God's Little Lessons on Life for Fathers
(0 86347 288 5)